Be Intentional: Estimating

*Developing the Right **Mindset** and **Habits** for Yourself and Your Team to Succeed with Estimating Property Insurance Claims*

By Jon Isaacson, *The Intentional Restorer*

Founder of The DYOJO
Host of The DYOJO Podcast

Jason & Mary —
It was so fun finally
meeting you in person — love what you do.
At Arcane Wayfinding. I hope we can find
a way to collaborate in the future. This
book targets insurance claims but
I believe the principles apply
to all construction.
Keep doing good
things!
JC

Table of Contents

Commandment 2 - Thou Canst Not Take Too Many Photos
Every estimate needs two things
Be consistent with your approach
The funny thing about photos (a rant)

Quote from David Baker, Home Estimating Services

Commandment 3 - Thou Shalt Label Thy Photos Descriptively
3D scanning for insurance claims
Improve profitability by reducing duplication
Helpful questions when considering new technologies

Quote from John Pastrava, President of RYZE Flood Solutions

Commandment 4 - Thou Shalt Utilize Thy F9 Notes
Communication is key to success
Contractors should be clear about their responsibilities

Common Estimating Issues

Commandment 5 - Thou Shalt Document Thy Initial Findings
12 hour update for mitigation
Loss narrative for repairs
Do it right
Do it efficiently
Do it excellently

The Four P's of the Blueprint for Success

Commandment 6 - Thou Shalt Update Thy Adjuster in Real Time and Document Consistently
Communication is a core issue
Clarity at the point of work initiation
Follow the rule of no surprises
Use the tools at your disposal

Quote from Raymond Tittmann, Managing Partner Tittman Weix

Commandment 7 - Thou Shalt Learn Thy Carrier's Guidelines
Low hanging fruit
Review your rejections
Naming conventions
Play the game with class and sass
Quantity over quality?
Are you trying hard enough?

Quote from Ben Justesen, President of Enlightened Restoration Solutions

Commandment 8 - Thou Shalt Know Thy Line Items (Apply Thyself to Understand the Process of Line Item Approvals)
Unleash the power of memorization
Macros
Cut and paste
Build your system to your vision
What is scope creep?

Recent Publications Featuring Articles from Jon Isaacson

Commandment 9 - Thou Shalt Know Thy Line Items (Thou Shalt Understand Thy Line Item Descriptions)
Internal reviews before external rejections
From estimate to production
Labor costs
Labor burden
Materials
Equipment
Overhead and profit

Quote from Annissa Coy, Owner of Firehouse Education

Commandment 10 - Thou Shalt Learn to Master the Trifecta of Service, Expedience and Accuracy
Service
Expedience
Accuracy

The DYOJO Podcast Audio & Visual Infotainment

Insurance Claims Estimating Mastery Starts with Knowing the Guidelines of Xactimate
The 10 Commandments of the Status Quo
Detached leaders enable cultures that harbor poor performers
Two questions that will help you be a better leader

Quote from Andrew McCabe, Owner of Claims Delegates

What Can We Do To Make It Better?
Feedback to Xactimate
Collaboration for industry advocacy

Property Restoration and Service Based Podcasts

Habits of Xactimate Estimating Proficiency
Poorly structured estimates show a lack of care and/or expertise
Structural habits will generate estimating consistency

How top-down or bottom-up informs our estimate structure
Setting your estimate apart from the status quo
Your habits demonstrate your professionalism

Fixing Bad Estimating Habits from Kirk Matthews

Help! Claims Review Shredded My Estimate
Estimate rejection response options
Simple data will help you drive change

Epilogue
Alternate book names
Same band, same sad tune?
The Bruce Lee mindset for business

Epilogue

About The Author

PREFACE

If I can do it, so can you.

How Did You Get Here?

U nless you grew up in the family business, you probably had never heard about property restoration until you arrived at your first interview. I remember my first interview. I thought I was going to be the next Gil Grissom. For those of you that don't know, there was this show, CSI: Crime Scene Investigation, that started in 2000. It made crime scene investigation really exciting.

The show wasn't the reason I wanted to go into the field, but it did help me combine my interest in law enforcement, science and the desire to do something good for the underdogs. Gil may also have inspired me to eventually grow a distinguished beard (although mine pales in comparison to Gerrett Stier's of The GMS Podcast fame).

I answered a newspaper advertisement. I'll pause there for a second - there used to be these things called the newspaper and...anyways, that's how one would job search in the 1900's (as my kids say). I found a print advertisement for carpet cleaning at a local franchise.

You may not have ever utilized a newspaper and at that point in time, I didn't realize that a franchise was a thing. I remember the owner, who had the longest legs and yet wore the shortest shorts, telling me about this mold remediation division that they were starting. He said that because I had a "background in science" I would really enjoy it.

I said, "Sign me up!" Little did I know I had just discovered a whole new world (cue music from Aladdin). This invitation onto the magic carpet was my introduction to an industry that I didn't know existed. Thankfully, I was also paired with a mentor who would become a lifelong friend. My manager, Denis Beaulieu, helped me to see the possibilities that this multifaceted industry has to offer.

The Power Of A Confident Leader

I had a fun opportunity to reminisce on some of the past with Mr. Beaulieu on Episode 15[1] of The DYOJO Podcast. Denis had learned Xactimate not that long before hiring me but he shared what he knew and the estimate structure that he had developed. Some of the best attributes of Denis as a leader were that he was confident in who he was and created opportunities for people to supplement his weaknesses.

In case you missed that plug, aspiring leaders take notes:

Be confident in who you are (strengths) and honest with who/ what you are not (weaknesses). This type of confidence will allow you to identify areas of need and resource solutions from within your team.

Allow your weaknesses to create opportunities for others to supplement your roles and responsibilities for the good of the team. This will help you to maximize what you are good at, help your team to grow and help engage individuals within your group.

As we built upon the process, I learned that it is important to set up the parameters and create freedom for others to contribute. I have heard that kids in a school yard play better when the boundaries are established[2]. In business, I have found this to be effective, wherein those in positions of leadership are responsible to establish the structure and define the organizational norms (culture) while allowing for team members to contribute with creativity.

This is a discussion for another book, but it's worth noting as we are talking about the **mindset** and **habits** which form the foundation for a successful individual and team strategy for estimating. Xactimate is a tool, you have to learn to use it. For me, this first came through copying the estimate structure, line items and methods from Denis. I would print out estimates and study them. I would cut and paste line items and then adjust the measurements.

William Mendoza shares, on The DYOJO Podcast Episode 13[3], the methods by which he taught himself Xactimate which included copying estimates from what he perceived to be successful restoration contractors. I learned early on that one of the most useful functions of Xactimate is that if you create an accurate sketch (see chapter on Commandment 1) you can extrapolate your measurements for square footage (SF), cubic footage (CF), linear feet (LF) and a host of other variations. The data that can be derived from a few inputs is helpful to all facets of property restoration, construction and insurance.

Growing With Xactimate

I believe Xactimate is a great tool for learning to think through the process of mitigation and repairs. Many contractors have developed skills in the hands-on aspects of the trades but they are often under developed in their business skills. Knowing how to estimate the work that you plan to do is key to building a successful business. It's not complicated but it is a skill set that you must **develop intentionally**.

For new contractors, Xactimate offers a tool that will help you create proposals based upon data and figures rather than just shooting from the hip or following your gut. I went from working in a franchise that did a heavy volume of insurance referral work to helping a general contractor start up a restoration division.

In this new company, we did not have Xactimate but I set up a rough price list within Quickbooks to follow the line item outlines I had learned while working for the team in yellow. RS Means is the "old school" way to gather normalized pricing by regions, so I referenced these printed manuals while developing our pricing strategy. It takes a lot of work to create a database like Xactimate, I have a lot of respect for what the Loveland's accomplished with Xactware.

You don't have to dig very deep in the interwebs to find contractors who will bad mouth Xactimate. You need to form your own opinions about the tool and understand it is a tool, if one cannot utilize the tool correctly - is that all the manufacturers fault? Another positive thing I will say about Xactimate is that the line item structure is transparent, anyone reading the estimate knows level-by-level, room-by-room and line-by-line the details of the proposal.

The Benefits Of Being An Independent

In this new role of developing a restoration division within an existing contracting firm, we were independent. We were not a part of the preferred vendor systems and we weren't using the tool prescribed by the industry czar's. I discovered that as an independent contractor you could still do insurance work and that you had more leverage to discuss what a fair-and-customary estimate would be.

The age-old question of whether you trade a potential high volume of work for lack of independence or maintain pricing autonomy with the reality that you may not get as much volume as the big players.

Estimating strategy is an ongoing discipline and improving your abilities requires intentionality. For this company and into my own, I developed the habit of pricing things at least three ways: 1) pricing based upon quantifiable data (line item pricing), 2) cost plus estimating and 3) subcontractor bids. As an estimator you need to round out your approach and not use any one tool as a crutch.

We will talk a lot about the pricing structures within Xactimate, so I won't touch on that here. Cost plus and subcontractor bids are important as you need to understand the labor rates for your area for various trades, materials, equipment and subcontractor pricing so that you can confirm what you are budgeting in Xactimate is keeping you in the game. It will also help you understand where there are gains and shortfalls within Xactimate pricing.

Xactimate is a great way to learn the format, structure and strategy of estimating but it should not be relied upon as the sole authority in creating accurate and profitable estimates for your organization. On the other hand, you cannot complain about the variances in the program if you do not understand those hard figures that we listed above.

Then The Recession Happened

I had my own business. It was not all unicorns and rainbows, but we were starting to gain steam. In Oregon, they say these financial impacts hit later and take longer to dig out of. We just like to do things at our own pace I guess.

In November of 2008, I can remember being booked and thinking this would be the first Christmas we weren't sweating. By February of 2009 the phone stopped ringing and all the work we had on the calendar had cancelled or the client was unable to be reached.

It was the worst of times professionally and incredibly challenging personally as we had a young family with four children to provide for. Yet, it was also some of the best times in our marriage, for our faith and as a family. I share some of those things in a self published article *Lessons*[4] if you want to hear more about that.

Rachel Stewart has a great saying on Episode 20 of The DYOJO Podcast[5], "Every crisis leads to opportunity." While that was hard to see in the moment and I was taking huge punches to the gut in my ego and self-worth as we fought through our struggles, it is true. If you are willing to apply your heart to what you observe, you will learn a lesson from what you see[6].

After doing anything and everything to find work, I finally had a call from one of the largest players in the property restoration ecosystem. Truth be told, they rejected me for the role of estimator because they weren't sure my experience would translate - gut punch. But they called about a week later with another opportunity. I wasn't starting over but I wasn't getting back into the same roles, responsibilities or salary that I had before.

A year of grinding it out on temp work, a jerky factory and a high needs retirement home, had prepared me to be thankful for the opportunity to be back in property restoration at any level.

The Origins Of This Manuscript

I have worked in some of the largest organizations in our business as well as in businesses as small as my own two-man operation. No matter how big or how small, the ability to consistently create accurate estimates is key to being successful in producing profitable work.

Estimates have an essential role in helping you build upon The Four P's of The Blueprint for Success. Strong estimating mindset and habits will help you:

Attract and keep good **people**, setting a baseline of accountability among the team which reduces bad hires and helps poor performers either improve or move on.

Provide resources to invest in your **process** so that you can identify issues, resolve them, repeat and build upon your success.

Create an outline for your **production** to be efficient and profitable by reducing scope creep and elevating the importance of clear communication within your team, with your client and with the carriers.

Enable your organization to make **progress** towards their goals.

If you think this is too loftily of a view of the role of estimating, let's extrapolate what the status quo mindset and habits lead to:

A roller coaster of turnover as the best people leave your organization and only those who don't have other options stay.

Inconsistent resources lead to friction as you constantly have to determine which never ending list of needs gets which fraction of your limited resources.

Unclear scopes lead to incomplete production plans which result in frustrated employees, upset subcontractors, wasted energy, resource drag, underwhelmed carriers and unhappy clients.

Too often we repeat the same tired speech at the end of the year, telling ourselves and our teams that, "This year is going to be different." Which may be well intentioned, but without intentionality business continues on a carousel of imbalance between vision, implementation and resolve.

This book is an outflow of my years of working in and writing about our industry. Much of this has culminated into my monthly column with Restoration and Remediation Magazine (R&R). Thanks to the brilliant Michelle Blevins, this column is titled *The Intentional Restorer*[7]. The concepts and principles are also what fuel The DYOJO Podcast[8] where we talk shop with business owners, entrepreneurs and professionals from the property restoration, construction and insurance communities. When we connect and collaborate, we can help each other to conquer our obstacles. We can shorten our DANG learning curve.

CHAPTER 1:

Is this a stupid book or a dumb book?

Why Should I Read This Stupid Book About A Stupid Program That Everyone Hates?

Good question.

Eloquently worded.

First, this book isn't stupid. Stupid means showing a great lack of intelligence or common sense. The goal of this book is to help you develop some common sense approaches to estimating in property restoration as a means of:

Career development
Team engagement
Organizational achievement
Process improvement
And other flashy business words

So, this book isn't stupid, technically it's dumb. Dumb, as an informal verb, means to, "Simplify or reduce the intellectual content of something so as to make it accessible to a larger number of people." In this sense, I would be rather encouraged to find you mention in your Google and/or Kindle (Amazon) reviews that this was, *"The dumbest book I ever read (all the way through) on this topic."*

When we make things more complicated than they ought to be, this is baroque.

Keys and Swords

If you plan to build a career in the property restoration space, Xactimate has become an essential tool for rendering services in this industry if you want to play the game. Love it or hate it, you need to be aware of what the estimating platform is and how to set yourself up for success with this resource.

If you are pursuing the keys to this kingdom, the freedom to drive down the highways of the property restoration career pathway with your hair blowing in the wind, you must develop the right **mindset** and **habits** to execute with Xactimate.

Like many tools, using it incorrectly can get you and others into needless trouble. Your trip down the career pathway will be trading one lemon for another and rather than the wind blowing in your hair (if you still have any), you will be picking bug fragments from your teeth.

Poor estimating in property restoration will tank a business. Bad habits and the wrong mindset will create tension between estimators, project managers and the employees in the field who are subsequently tasked with making a crappy estimate work.

In too many organizations, the end line workers are blamed for issues that start further up the line. Managers are quick to call out under-performing technicians but hesitant to dig beyond the symptoms to fix the core issues. If you are in leadership, make sure you understand the difference between effects and causes.

Thankfully, you don't have to be special to clutch the sword from this industry's stone, but you will want to cultivate some core principles if you want to wield it effectively. As 35 year industry veteran, Mark Cornelius, says, "Learn how to use the hammer to its utmost capabilities. Become the most proficient person on the planet with that hammer."

Releasing the sword from the stone is simply a matter of making the monthly or annual payments to Verisk (the parent company of Xactware, the creators of Xactimate). Anyone with a laptop, a credit card and Internet Explorer can access Xactimate Online.

Funny story, when I recently incorporated Xactimate Online with a new company, I attempted to login to Xactimate and kept getting a prompt to download Silverlight which I already had. I called support and they told me I must utilize the tool in Internet Explorer.

According to this person, the tool only works in Internet Explorer. I asked the person on the other line when they would be sending me an AOL free trial internet disk. They did not get the reference. If you don't, you will have to Google it for yourself.

Doesn't it amaze you how slow many large companies are to adapt to changes in the market and seem unwilling to spend money to improve the customer experience? We can say this in unison about X company that we all have issues with but are we willing to aim those same barbs at our own companies? Often you are what you hate.

If You Are New To The Industry Or Just Starting Out Your Career:

Do yourself a favor and form your own opinions.

This will be difficult but, tune out the 20% of the haters who are burned out and have nothing but negative things to say about the tools available to them. The 20% on the other extreme, the kool-aid drinkers who are so protective of the system that they shield it from any criticism, can also be troublesome.

Those who camp in the extremities often have little to offer to those who want to explore their opportunities. They have formed their opinions and their life's mission is to defend their perspectives regardless of what anyone else has to offer. Your mission, should you choose to accept it, is to form your own opinion as this will be essential to developing a proper mindset.

Learn something from everyone.

There will be many people that you meet throughout your career and for whom their only contribution is to show you very clearly how NOT to do something. You will have co-workers, managers and even executives who are the definition of the *Peter Principle* - those who have been promoted beyond the point of their competency.

These people were promoted for a reason, and this tells you something about the system and the organizations that they work in. If you are willing to keep an open mind, there is always something to learn that can help you on your path. Whatever you do, don't allow others to steal the joy of the journey that is possible in property restoration with their avarice, burnout or their incompetence.

Create a pathway for success

This book will help you **form a mindset** and **establish habits** for executing a pathway for success as you continue to build your career within insurance claims response and repairs.

There are opportunities everywhere, if you will buckle in with a growth mindset, we can teach you the fundamentals of driving in the fast lane in the property restoration industry. We can help you maintain the hunger and drive that will release the sword from the stone.

For Those Who Have Experience...

If you have been in the business for a while and are ready to take your career to the next level:

Maintain your own perspective

Hopefully you have been able to form your own opinions and you have learned a bit of something from everyone. Unlike those who are new to the industry, you have seen the highs and the lows, and to your credit - you are still here. Maintain your own perspective.

Celebrate your path

Endurance is worth celebrating and it will be necessary to continue your way upward. Property restoration can be brutal, especially if you don't have the right mindset and have learned self-destructive habits. If you are frustrated, know that you are not alone and The DYOJO is here to help. Endurance produces character and character produces hope.

Use your tools, before they use you

You know enough to know that Xactimate is more than a tool, it is a key resource with a significant presence in the bulk of the organizations who operate within the property damage response and repairs services for insurance claims. Like any tool in your toolbox, learn to use it the way it was intended and it will unlock doors for you as a professional.

My goal is to help you build upon your growth mindset and optimize your habits to position yourself to **continue to create value** for yourself, the organization you work with, the various carriers and your clients.

If You Are A Manager...

Or a person in a position of leadership (PIAPOL[9]) working to help others to develop their skills in this industry, here are a few things to keep in mind:

Help yourself by helping others

Thank you. The greatest calling and highest return on investment comes from those in a position of leadership who understand their roles and responsibilities revolve around making those in their care better.

It's one thing to develop yourself and build a career, it's another level of growth for yourself and your team when you assist them in **reaching their full potential**. You are doing good things.

We get paid for what we document

This book will help managers to **communicate and empower** new employees as well as those team members who are ready to grow in their roles. It is helpful for all employees to understand the role of Xactimate and how documentation is at the core of how we get paid as restoration contractors.

It's hard for many to understand that we don't get paid for what we do, we get paid for what we can document that we did. Strong documentation leads to a solid estimate which leads to a profitable payout.

Helping everyone in your organization to understand how a typical property restoration estimating / billing is composed helps front line employees to understand the importance of their documentation from the field.

It also shows them a pathway to career opportunities, for example, if you do well with documentation at this current phase there will be opportunities for you to understand and excel with the documentation at the next level.

As you climb the ladder, the documentation is never less, it is always more.

What this book isn't

This book is NOT a step-by-step guide for using Xactimate nor is it the definitive resource for mastering estimating in property restoration. You will not read this book and then be able to jump in the vehicle and start driving down the winding roads of the insurance landscape at top speed.

This book will help you learn how to operate the system, understand the rules of the road and set up habits that relate to the best practices for estimating.

This book will help sharpen your senses for taking on greater challenges in your professional development. The value of this book is in setting the right growth mindset for approaching insurance repairs and developing habits that will lead you down the path of success with the resources available to you.

If you are new to Xactimate, this book will help you to form a much better understanding of the framework for clear and consistent estimates.

If you have been using Xactimate for a while but have been frustrated with poor results, this book will help you correct many of those bad habits that commonly plague poorly structured teams.

If you are an adjuster or a claims review professional, this will help you understand the estimating dynamics and will be a tool that will help you better converse with restoration professionals.

If one of your responsibilities is to train estimators and/ or build a team, this book will help you to present the foundational information to your team members and will provide them with resources that will supplement your hands on training.

Paying it forward

With hard work, good mentors and enough smarts to seize upon the chances presented to me, I grew from a technician to managing multiple operations for companies large and small.

Xactimate is one component of a much larger picture, but by discussing the **mindset** and **habits** that will help you achieve success with this tool, we will also discuss how those core principles relate to so many aspects of sound business.

Estimating is foundational to success in service based industries which include property restoration, construction, auto repairs, plumbing, electrical, adjusting, sales and many more.

Establishing a culture that will thrive in today's ever challenging market requires employee engagement, team development and process improvement.

When we invest in The Four P's of The Blueprint for Success[10] - **P**eople, **P**rocess, **P**roduction and **P**rogress, we will place ourselves in the running to achieve our goals.

CHAPTER 2:

The 3 R's of Mastering
Xactimate for Beginners

Success in property restoration for insurance claims starts with building a solid foundation for mastering the tools of the trade. In the world of insurance claims, professionals who seek to create career opportunities for themselves by providing services for water and fire damage repairs to structures will need to familiarize themselves with an estimating program called Xactimate.

Before we get into some of the keys to success with this tool, we first need to answer, what is Xactimate? In a white paper titled Xactimate: The History & The Future from Actionable Insights, Mark Whatley[15] writes,

> *"Starting in 1989, Xactware pioneered a scientific approach to providing building cost data for the restoration ecosystem. From the outset, Xactware's primary function has been to report market prices based upon industry surveys and recent transactions that have occurred."*

Over the last three decades, Xactimate has become the standardized estimating platform for the property restoration and insurance adjusting communities. Xactimate skills are at a premium whether you are an adjuster, a claims professional or a restoration contractor. This program is the claims tool understood and preferred by insurance carriers as well as third-party administrators (TPAs).

If you haven't already heard about the program, you won't have to go far to find those who speak disparagingly about Xactimate. As I noted in the opening chapter, the best thing you can do is form your own opinion. There are plenty of opportunities in this industry and there is money to be made by a variety of means and methods.

Whether you are starting your career in property restoration, looking to advance in the industry or a contractor entertaining the idea of utilizing Xactimate to streamline your estimating process, approach this as you would any other tool and learn its capabilities before you decide how you view its efficacy.

Your responsibility to the process.

In this book we will explore foundational topics that will be of use to new estimators, manager's responsible for training estimators, and business owners who want to better understand how to set up standard operating procedures (SOPs) for their organization.

Xactimate is the estimating platform. It was built and intended to be a tool to assist contractors and carriers in communicating clearly to each other the details of the loss so that a scope of work can be assembled, understood in a common "language", expedite the approval process and thereby get the wheels turning to restore clients impacted by perils covered in their insurance policies.

The goal is to ensure that the policyholder is restored to pre-loss conditions, no more and no less. Clients and contractors who attempt to gain the system are potentially committing fraud. Carriers, adjusters, TPA's and claims professionals who attempt to whittle the estimate to twigs are short changing the client.

What Is Program Work?

If your company does "program" work, this means that there will be additional layers of review that you will be subject to as an estimator. It also means that your organization has made certain concessions that you will not be able to battle against.

Some of the most widely utilized third party administrators include:

Contractor Connection

Alacrity Solutions - merger between Alacrity and Nexxus

Sedgewick

Innovation Property Network (IPN)

Code Blue

If you visit online forums, attend industry conferences or meet with insurance contractors, you will inevitably hear someone complain about program work. The common retort to the supposed nuisance of doing program work is that TPA's provide a level of volume that otherwise might be unattainable by a contractor that is not a part of the preferred vendor system.

I would encourage you to decide for yourself what is best for you, as opposed to allowing others to influence your opinions. Program work will keep you on your toes and will require you to learn the nuances of various carrier requirements as well as the depth of the concessions that your company has made with the carriers that you will be working with.

You have to become a student of the game that you are playing. We discuss approaches to claims reviews and rejections later in this book in a chapter titled, *Help, Claims Review Shredded my Estimate.*

What Does It Mean To Be Independent?

If your company has remained "independent" of the programs, this means that you are not beholden to a special set of rules. You still have to know what the adjusters and carriers you work with expect but you are not required to jump through additional hoops and/or processes that are inherent to the preferred vendor (aka program) estimators.

You may face frustration when a project you really want to be a part of is "stolen" by a program contractor. Preferred vendor typically applies to a contractor who is part of a TPA program, someone who has inked "a deal with the devil" according to many independents.

Contractor Connection (CC) states that it is a network of over 6,000 contractors from the United States and Canada. This network is much larger than even the largest companies in the property restoration landscape. Many companies have adopted the mindset, "If you can't beat them, join them," which is the nature of the relationship between many contractors and CC.

Independent contractors have to find ways to generate revenue that is directed to the program vendors through their agreements with the third party administrators. Every decision has its pros and cons as well as its resulting consequences. Typically program, or preferred, vendors receive a higher volume of claims, which leads to higher revenue overall but also creates challenges for profitability.

On the other hand, independent vendors retain more of their autonomy in their operations as well as a stronger position for achieving the margins that they seek, but they also have to find other avenues to generate work outside of the largest aggregator in the industry. Many independent contractors end up utilizing cumbersome and/or expensive options such as lead generators or paying for leads from local plumbers.

Some of the peer-to-peer networking groups available to property restoration contractors include (further details found in Chapter 16):

Alliance of Independent Restorers (AIR)

International Cleaning and Restoration Association (ICRA)

National Organization of Restoration and Remediation Professionals (NORRP)

The Restoration Association

Restoration Industry Association (RIA)

Restoration Rebels

Preparing yourself to explore career opportunities as an Xactimate estimator

To start this journey, if you are new to Xactimate we have three tips, which we discuss in the next chapter, that will help you begin your voyage towards mastering the best practices for this estimating platform. We will discuss foundational principles as well as some of the next level tools that are available to estimators who are intentional about improving their skills.

Educational Resources For Xactimate Include:

This book. Share it on your social media and tell your friends about all the things that you have learned!

Actionable Insights provides a monthly Xactimate price list update summary to help keep you informed on what has changed within this resource.

Enlightened Restoration Solutions offers Xactimate training courses and a Pricing feedback webinar from Ben Justesen.

Xactware provides a variety of training options to pursue Xactimate certification.

The DYOJO has a resource page for Property Restoration

which includes articles and videos on Xactimate success

A Word Of Encouragement From Jeff Moore

Jeff Moore, President of American Technologies, Inc. (ATI[16]), shares what he would tell his young self if he could go back in time to drop some knowledge regarding Xactimate:

> My first order of business would be to get myself certified in both levels 1, 2, and 3 (of Xactimate) as soon as physically possible.
>
> I would encourage you, young Jeff, to get involved with the industry, locally, regionally and nationally plus attend the Xactware conference if your company will allow for this.
>
> And if you, Jeff, plan on staying in the industry for the duration, I would encourage you to seek your training certification. You might be thinking, why try and become a certified estimator? It will force you to stay current with the software and you will be VALUABLE to your employer, to your community and most importantly to your adjuster clients.

Selling Yourself To Achieve Your Goals

While this may sound risqué, this is the mindset that you must have if you want to make your career growth goals a reality. While the keys to an organization's success are investing in their people, process, production and progress, you have to do this on an individual level as well. Invest in yourself, your process, your production and your progress.

Unfortunately, not all business owners and/or mid to high level leaders who hold the purse strings of the company believe in investing in their people to the degree that Jeff Moore discusses above. Most companies will have some level of training, or it may be more like "training", but you will have to advocate for yourself and pursue ongoing education.

You are responsible for your professional development. In order to have your company invest in these programs you likely will have to learn to sell the value to them. Perhaps this quote from Jeff will be helpful in that endeavor. Estimators are sales people, you have to sell yourself everyday to your clients, you will also have to continue to sell yourself to your own company to align support with your goals.

Whether you are able to attend the big events for networking and training or not, there are many ways to pursue technical training as well as develop your proficiency in the skills relevant to growing your property restoration career. You have to own your responsibility to develop intentionally.

CHAPTER 3:

Learning from Rejection, Repetition and Relationships

I f you are going to enter into the world of estimating structural damage mitigation and repairs, you will likely cut your teeth with a company that relies heavily on Xactimate as their estimating platform.

This tool is the de-facto resource for property restoration contractors as well as the platform used by "the other side", being the carrier reviewers, third party administrators (TPAs), third party consultants (TPCs) and adjusters.

Before you can succeed with Xactimate you need to be prepared for what we at The DYOJO call, *The Three R's*. These are the foundational pillars of your growth mindset with regards to Xactimate, and many other obstacles, they are:

R1 - Learning from Rejection

R2 - Learning from Repetition

R3 - Learning from Relationships

Tip #1: You Must Learn from Rejection

Even though the Xactimate platform is standardized, there are many approaches to the claims writing process. Often the best way to structure your estimate is **either from the top down or from the bottom up**. Literally, you can either start your estimate, and the sequence of line items from which it will be built, from the highest point of the damage or in the reverse, you can start from the floor and work your way up.

This is your first habit. Approach every loss the same way so that you help ensure that you don't miss items. When an estimator is missing valid work scopes and sequences, they are leaving legitimate money on the table. Even though you can supplement "upon discovery" it is important that you don't get into the bad habit of being lazy with your data capture at the outset of a project. Habits fuel success.

Knowing the types of adjusters / reviewers:

If you write an estimate, you are going to get reviewed and you are going to get rejected, it's part of the process. In so far as it depends on you, work to create relationships based on trust with the carriers, adjusters and reviewers that you most frequently work with.

For those who are new to insurance, as well as your clients who are likely experiencing their first insurance claim, a common mistake is confusing an insurance agent with an insurance adjuster.

Who Reviews An Estimate?

Field Adjuster

Those adjusters who physically go to a loss to see and document the claim on behalf of the carrier. Field adjusters have the experience of having visited claims, they understand the full 4D experience of an active loss, of helping a client through a disaster to their home or business and have a broader understanding of what it takes to navigate a claim. Field adjusters can interpret the letter of the law (the policy language) as well as the intent of the law (the grey areas of those that apply to the physical loss).

For The DYOJO Podcast Episode 23 we have a good conversation with Kirk Matthews who shares many of the ins and outs of working with adjusters. He has worked both as a "captive" adjuster with some of the largest carriers in the business and as an independent representing various insurance companies Whether you are new to the process or need some guidance with adjuster relationships, this is a good episode to help you improve your perspective of what "the other side" does.

Desk adjuster

Many carriers have adjusters who review estimates from a remote claims center, this is becoming more of the norm. These professionals do not go to the loss site and may have never visited a claim so their claims understanding is typically based on what they have learned from their one dimensional claims training.

To be an adjuster, as opposed to a claims professional, these representatives should have undergone the process of achieving their adjuster designation. As Kirk Matthews shares on The DYOJO Podcast Episode 23, you may be working with a seasoned adjuster who is at the helm or someone just starting out their career in insurance.

Claims reviewer

If the carrier is part of a third party administrator (TPA) program, your estimate will likely be reviewed by a claims reviewer prior to being submitted or reviewed by the carrier's representatives. Claims professionals and/or reviewers have not completed the training and do not carry the designation that adjusters have.

Claims professionals review estimates based upon the parameters of the agreement between the carrier, the contractor and/or the client. Claims reviewers only interpret the letter of the law, often down to the very finely printed details.

Tip #2: You Must Learn from Repetition

Xactimate is designed for the straight forward losses. While we may disagree on the percentage of claims that are "typical", there are going to be losses that break with the norm. For the majority of your losses, once you have a loss format that has been accepted you can either create a macro or cut and paste that format.

In my opinion, macros can be more work than they are worth but there are plenty of YouTube videos on how to construct these tools. I prefer to memorize the codes and line items that you utilize most frequently and utilize prior approved estimates as standards for future claims. When you develop your understanding of how Xactiamte is set up, you will find it becomes more user friendly with repetition, but you have to first challenge yourself to memorize certain things. The search function is helpful as you begin this process.

Understanding the Xactimate code structure:

For example, seasoned estimators will always refer to carpet as FCC. What is FCC? Floor Covering Carpet. Now that you know this sequence, what do you think FCV is? If you guessed Floor Covering Vinyl, you are correct. Hardwood flooring is FCW. Line items associated with carpet are likely going to be in the FCC group.

If you have to replace the padding, you are going to use FCC and then you can try p-a-d and sure enough you find FCC PAD is carpet padding. But, don't stop there, you have to read the line item description and ensure you are using the correct padding. If your carpet pad is greater quality than a 6 pound stock (the most common) you may need to utilize another line item.

It is not essential to be versed in the construction process to estimate with Xactimate but it definitely helps. Google can teach you a lot and even seasoned estimators have to look things up from time-to-time, but nothing beats getting out into the field and even doing some of the work to elevate your comprehension of how structures work so that you can construct your estimate with a greater degree of precision.

Most of your mitigation line items are going to be found in WTR. What is a dehumidifier going to be under? You start to type d-e-h-u and that doesn't bring anything up, unless you search. But you soon discover its WTR DHM and an air mover is WTR DRY. As noted before, read the line items. There are various sizes of dehumidifiers and types of air movers.

As noted with the carpet pad, which is what code _ _ _ - _ _ _, don't just type in DHM and walk away. Look up the line item detail and understand the difference between the categories of equipment to ensure you are charging for the correct unit.

Residential work in particular is often very similar as the sources for a loss result from a consistent short list of culprits such as a toilet overflow, water heater failure, leaking ice maker line, etc. The majority of your water damage work will be bathrooms, kitchens or utility rooms. As such, you can set up profiles in your estimating bank of similar losses to use as a reference when you are composing estimates or you can set up macros.

Where rejection and repetition meet collaboration

If you work for, or are building, a strong organization, then you will have an internal process for reviewing estimates before they go out to any level of review. As a growth minded professional and as a person in leadership building a culture, the collaboration that comes from reviewing each other's estimates should be a net positive. Internal review should be quick and consistent, the process will help offset deep cuts and embarrassment by estimators.

As an estimator who is learning the platform, pay attention to what you are getting rejected for.

Refer to our later chapter *Help, Claims Review Shredded My Estimate* which is also an article in R&R as well as a video on The DYOJO Youtube channel.

Try to not repeat the same mistakes with the same adjusters and/or carriers. Every carrier has their general rules as well as their idiosyncrasies.

For example, one carrier will want content manipulation

written in Xactimate as CON LAB, which is an hourly charge for manipulation, whereas another will want to see it as CON ROOM, which is a fee set up by the size of the room. It should only take one rejection for you to understand and remember which carrier prefers the line item one way or the other.

Many estimators leave legitimate money on the table by not developing their content line items beyond these two options. Money can be made in contents, that is why there are several successful companies who specialize in this niche service. As with any scope of work, think through the labor sequences, the materials involved, the transportation, manipulation and storage options. This could be another book entirely. Annissa Coy, the queen of contents, shares a lot of good information in her column with Restoration and Remediation (R&R) magazine.

Tip #3: You Must Learn from Relationships

Get to know your local adjusters. For those losses that break from the normal, what many perceive as an in-and-out claim, make contact early and often with your local adjusters. You will learn what they see as simple approvals and what their idiosyncrasies are for the carrier they work for. Once you know the adjuster, make their job easier.

If you haven't already learned this principle, making someone else's life simpler is a great strategy for career and professional development. Make this your mindset. When you make your boss's job easier, you will get noticed. When you make your client's life simpler, you will create an exceptional experience. When you make an adjuster's life less painful, you open the doors for a strong professional relationship.

Try not to contact an adjuster for every little change but rather have your items in order so that you can discuss the claim and make a reasonable request that serves the client as well as meets the guidelines of the carrier. This goes back to capturing the loss details on the front end, writing a thorough and accurate estimate and then communicating discoveries of additional damages during the execution of the claim are all important to developing good habits.

While you want to build enduring professional relationships it is important to keep things in perspective. When you are starting out, be careful with adjusters and consultants who are too friendly. Be professional and set an expectation of professionalism, don't be lured into a potential trap because someone appears to be nice. Maintain your process for documenting the claim, getting approvals in writing and communicating throughout the process.

I don't want to encourage people to be cynical, but you must treat every claim as though it were your worst in the sense that you have your file dialed in. If you have ever been to court, it is an arduous process of combing through the fine details of your documentation. There is nothing better than having your affairs in order and presenting a sound counter to someone who wants to speak ill of your team and your process.

A few rules for professional relationships

Because I hope for this to be a book that reaches new estimators and I have had many of these conversations with young professionals that we coach, I think it is important to share a few ground rules for developing relationships in the insurance realm. Anyone who has been in the industry for time will have some level of pessimism. Like we said, form your own opinions, but that doesn't mean you should disregard some of this battle tested wisdom.

For us to have a professional "relationship" it must be **mutually beneficial**. If deals are being made, they should be made in a manner that is fair to all parties. I see many new contractors caught in situations where they have given too much and have little left to give when additional concessions are requested. They think they are playing the game but they are being played.

Think of concessions in the mindset of a courtroom where **precedence** is being established. An adjuster or consultant may ask for a concession that seems reasonable, but by making this deal are you setting a precedent that you can maintain with future losses and/or in other areas of your estimate?

On the flip side of this coin, if you are not making the effort to communicate early and often with the carrier and their representatives, you cannot cry wolf at the end of the process when they rip your invoice to shreds.

Be professional, be polite but don't get played.

Also, the insurance agent is not the adjuster. Update and inform the agent as a means of customer service and securing future work but understand that the adjuster has the authority over the claims process. The agent is the salesperson and customer representative, so they can help you advocate for the client, but they do not have authority to negotiate claims outcomes.

This is often the rule with property managers as well as they represent the owner to a degree but may not have final authority. Make sure you understand who is paying the bill and who has authority to approve the scope of work as well as change orders. Get all of the various stakeholders involved with the claim identified, documented and properly updated to their level of involvement in the project.

Digging beneath the surface may also uncover some opportunities. For example, I had a property manager that had a set limit on what they could approve in-house. Previously I had lost several competitive bids or delayed the process because my estimates were above their local authority. When we discussed the threshold, I broke our estimates down into scopes and made some concessions for the volume of work. It paid off quite well as we significantly increased our mitigation, repairs and carpet cleaning work at that location.

Episodes of The DYOJO Podcast[17] discussing carrier relations:

Episode 1 - David Princeton of Advocate Claim Services discusses understanding the basics of policy language and limits as you construct your estimates.

Episode 6 - Raymond Tittmann of Tittmann Weix discusses the importance of discussing the claim early and often with the carrier so that you can work together to assist the insured.

Episode 9 - Mark Whatley of Actionable Insights discusses approaching adjusters with humility to discuss reaching a better outcome through clearer estimating practices.

Episode 10 - This is the first of the Pro vs. Joe series where we are walking a company new to property restoration through the nuances of insurance claims.

Episode 13 - William Mendoza of Rockland Restoration talks about his process of going line by line to teach himself Xactimate.

Episode 23 - Kirk Matthews of Oregon Valley and Coast Claim Service shares tips for maximizing your relationship with adjusters.

Xactimate best practices for claims estimating

It is helpful to have a consultant or mentor, whether this is an internal resource or someone you pursue from outside your company. There are helpful YouTube videos, independent training programs as well as courses that you can take. Don't let fear prevent you from reaching out to someone through email, LinkedIn, or for coffee. For most professionals in the industry, mastery has come through trial and error. If you want to survive and succeed in the insurance property claims industry, you must learn from rejection, repetition and relationships.

The goal of this book is to compile the information I have shared over the years through The DYOJO, The DYOJO Podcast and my monthly column, *The Intentional Restorer*. I have updated information, added content to the chapters and included insights from friends in the industry. This is meant to be a tool that will help estimators grow in their mindset and execution with regards to communicating the story of the loss.

As we say on The DYOJO Podcast, INOFtainment (information and entertainment) to help you shorten your DANG learning curve.

Whether you are new to the industry or responsible for helping others develop their skills, you will find our podcast within the podcast, Pro vs. Joe[18] to be a helpful resource. Myself and Bryan Close discuss his companies transition from primarily working for property managers to focusing on water and fire damage insurance repairs.

In many ways these videos and audio episodes are a master class in career development for growth minded property restoration, construction and insurance professionals.

Inights From An Xactimate Pro

Kirk Matthews, Senior Multi-Line Independent Adjuster with Oregon Valley and Coastal Claim Services[19], shares 5 simple keys to elevating your estimating game:

If you are an adjuster, ask a lot of questions. If you're newer to the process and have limited practical experience, reach out to trusted contractors to inquire what it takes to actually get this type of job done.

If you are a restorer, ask a lot of questions. Don't hesitate or be scared to ask your adjuster what are the red flags for the carrier that they represent as well as their preferred estimate structure. As you learn to work with adjusters and carriers, create a cheat sheet of do's and don't to watch out for on each project.

Nothing is better than rolling your sleeves up and doing some manual labor yourself. I learn so much by actually doing even small projects around my own home.

Get out in the field and observe the restoration

work being done. When was the last time as an adjuster or restorer that you visited a jobsite? Go to a jobsite while the work is in progress, and see what the operation looks like. Construction often is a lot of manual labor, including mundane and repetitive actions such as hauling buckets of debris, hanging large sheets of drywall or finding the right angles for replacing baseboard trim.

Reach out to your peers. Review their estimates and have them do the same for you. How do other professionals skin that cat? You may discover some new approaches or industry tricks for key gains such as using 8 line items to do a drywall patch rather than following the status quo of just using the labor minimum

CHAPTER 4:

*The 10 Commandments of
Xactimate Estimating Success*

W hy do entrepreneurs get into property restoration? Often it is because someone has the hairbrained idea that there is "easy money" at the end of the insurance rainbow. Or like many of us, you answered an ad or were encouraged by a friend to apply and found that there was an opportunity to make some money and eventually, maybe even a career.

If you know the rough story of the 10 Commandments, you know some guy named Moses went up the mountain and came back with two stone tablets that carried the words of God for the people. If you are old enough, Charelton Heston may be the face that you see due to his role in the classic movie by the same name. Perhaps you are younger and have seen the cartoon version titled *The Prince of Egypt*.

Many restoration professionals complain that the estimating landscape is desert wasteland that continues to suffer from the **drought of profits** manufactured by their oppressors, the insurance carriers and their enforcers, the Third Party Administrators (TPAs).

Fight as the good and ethical contractors may, they cannot loosen themselves from the **bonds of the system** created by the powers that be, such that Xactiamte has become an implement of abuse rather than a tool of the trades.

Well intentioned estimators try to learn **the secret ways of Xactware** but struggle to interpret what the burning bush is trying to tell them while they selectively follow the segments of the stone tablets that suit their purposes.

Contractors feel the pressure of facing the Red Sea but struggle to find a way to part the raging waters of **claims review** so that they can pass safely to the promised land.

For those just beginning their journey in estimating insurance claims, you will find our *Three R's of Mastering Xactimate for Beginners* (also covered in this book) to be a helpful baseline for success when attempting to traverse the property restoration landscape.

The cloud of mystery that surrounds the de facto industry estimating standard serves to scare and confuse many, but with the help of our cleverly composed 10 Commandments for Xactimate Estimating Success, you can develop the right mindset and form habits that will assist you in reaching your goals.

A brief note on TPCs

As you progress to larger losses, you will cross paths with Third Party Consultants (TPCs). JS Held and Young & Associates are two of the largest outfits which are frequently hired by the carrier to review a claim. One of the points of contention for many contractors is that it is one thing to discuss claim parameters and concessions on the front end, or start, of a claim but it is quite another scenario when estimates are scrutinized on the back end after the work has been completed.

At the time of writing this book, I have recorded an episode with a third party consultant who I met while we both worked for the same restoration company. It likely will be episode 26 of The DYOJO Podcast and you will learn about opportunities "on that side of the fence" as well as some nuggets for seeing things from their perspective.

Estimating in property restoration for insurance claims is so much more than putting numbers to paper and praying that your project goes well. Hope is not a strategy. You need to develop a good mindset and positive habits for estimating that will help you communicate, document and defend your work under any level of scrutiny. Learn to tell the story of the loss.

Unfortunately, you can do everything right and still be in a drawn out process. Life is not guaranteed to be fair. Contractors should always have their documentation structured in such a way that it will stand the test of scrutiny. Easier said than done, and I know many professionals who can share stories of misconduct, but do your part to play from ahead.

Communicate with the carrier early and often.

Get approvals in writing.

If you know this will be a large loss, ask the carrier what the threshold is for bringing in a third party consultant and ask who their preferred vendor is.

Provide scope of work and pricing updates along the way with documented approvals.

If you are going to charge your client the price regardless of what the carrier agrees to, be sure that the client is clear on this approach and this is outlined in your contract.

NOTE: These "10 Commandments" were released at the end of 2018 as an article that quickly rose to become the second most viewed web exclusive article for Restoration and Remediation Magazine (R&R). I could have retired on that accomplishment alone, but because I am a glutton for punishment I continued to write mediocre content to help professionals such as yourself.

I combined those insights with *Habits for Xactimate Estimating Success*, which was the 6th most popular web exclusive in 2019 (humble brag), and new content, including input from friends and peers in our industry, which is now compiled in this format to help you on your property restoration journey.

Remember, my goal is that upon completing this book, you will mention in your Google and/or Kindle (Amazon) review that this was, "*The dumbest book I ever read (all the way through) on this topic.*"

Lessons Learned From The Xactimate Program Estimating Trenches

David Smith[20], currently recovering from program work, shares six tips that will help estimators to master the estimate review process:

Know the story of the loss and communicate that in your estimate through the opening statement and F9 notes.

Understand your customers needs and what it will take to restore them to pre-loss conditions.

Know the estimate structure that meets the carrier's expectations and the nuances of the adjuster you are working with.

Understand how the loss is going back together, compose your estimate in a way that communicates your plan both to the adjuster as well as for your production team.

Involve your resources on how they will handle the loss, know the unique attributes of your in house labor and subcontractors.

Review your estimate and get a second pair of eyes checking your estimate prior to sending the document for review.

NOTE: I was going to ask for your permission to make a comment, but since this is my book, I'm going to make a big-boy decision and comment without confirmation of your approval. It is a shame that good people like David Smith go unrecognized, over-utilized and ejected from our industry.

I will be sharing some of that story in my next book on culture[21], which is a collaborative effort with many of the contributors in this book and from The DYOJO Podcast.

If You Are In A Position Of Leadership:

But, in the meantime, if you are in a position of leadership, take a closer look at the quality of the people you have in your organization. I can guarantee you have hidden gems who have demonstrated the quality of their character, their contributions to the organization and their zeal to develop, but they do it in a manner that isn't as flashy as those who "play the game".

Stop losing good people by being a ding-bat. Be intentional with your people, your process, your production and your progress. Invest in your people and you will see exhilarating returns on that investment.

If You Are An Employee Feeling Like You Are Getting Overlooked And Undervalued:

Some people have a wrong view of themselves and their contributions. If you have a bloated sense of your importance you will be a manager soon (sarcasm...and yet, an unfortunate reality). I want to speak to the "David's" out there, those who put the team first, who are grinding, doing things the right way, being efficient and even excellent, even if the bosses don't see it that way. Some things to consider:

First, life is a game. You don't have to play by everyone else's rules but you should be smart enough to understand what they value and how they perceive the workplace. In grasping this you will see how you can better position yourself to do the things that matter as well as decide whether you want to be a part of an organization or work for leadership that values those things. One side note, it's probably similar in other companies as well - so you may want to take at least a second look into whether you can make it work where you are.

A company should expect and value that you are honest, work hard and are willing to learn. If you come to work everyday with these three traits fully engaged, you will be valuable to any team. Unfortunately, honest, hard work and the hunger for knowledge do not mean the same thing for everyone.

Refer to the first lesson you must learn above. When you are the smaller entity, with less leverage, it is silly to think that the organization will adapt to you. You have to decide what it looks like and if you are willing to adapt to the organization.

This doesn't mean you give up the pursuit of making something better from the inside, but you must earn your voice and learn to use your voice to make strategic changes along the way.

At some point you have to test your value and determine who and where your efforts are best applied. While I have never placed chasing the money as my first priority, and I have turned down some lucrative offers (because I am such a baller), money is how we pay our bills and feed our families.

I learned early on from a mentor of my wife's that you should always be applying and interviewing for job opportunities. You want to keep yourself relevant, your interview skills on point and keep your options open. This doesn't mean you take every offer, but be aware of what is out there.

Take a few risks and apply for things that you don't yet qualify for. By doing so, if you get anywhere in the process you learn what it would take to position yourself for those roles and responsibilities that you are interested in pursuing.

Keep these things in mind:

Make a few small changes to play the game better without compromising your values. Think through what it would look like to position yourself to change the current perception of your value.

Stand up for yourself and say no once in a while. If other people expect that you will do all of the crap work, take the crap hours and don't give back then you are not in a partner-ship with management or your fellow employees (refer to *A Few Rules for Professional Relationships* in Chapter 3).

When you decide it's time to pursue the next thing, do your best to find the best fit in alignment with your values, the culture you want to be a part of and the best prospects for short as well as long term growth. There is more to growing your career, professional development and building wealth than your paycheck.

It may sound cynical, but I don't believe in the adage, "Do something you love and you will never work another day in your life." I think this is BS and sets a lot of people up to be disenchanted with work and life.

I believe you can find something that you love, or at least something that engages your passions, skills and abilities, in every organization. If you find what fuels you, you can operate in a way that fulfills you and provides value both to your organization and those whom you work with.

CHAPTER 5:

Estimating with Xactimate
- Commandment 1

Thou Shalt Sketch Accurately.

R egardless of the tools that you use, make sure that you get your sketch right. An accurate sketch is the key to creating a solid Xactimate estimate. Arguably this is the greatest feature of Xactimate as once the sketch is created elements of the estimating process can be approached from so many different angles.

Those who have used the platform understand the options for estimating from the sketch. This is a unique feature for scenarios such as:

If you are only replacing a certain wall

Creating blocks (B) for custom elements within a room

Line out an area (A) to help you eliminate quantities from existing totals

Then there is the carrier favorite of automatically deducting square footage of doors and windows from calculations

On location sketching

Sketching from the site is one of the best ways to ensure you get odd corners and turns in a unique layout accurately as well as capture all of your line items. One of the downsides to estimating from the field is having enough space to layout your estimating gear.

A good compromise is to get the basic structure together from the field and then dial in the details offsite in a more comfortable setting where you can spread out your documentation for reference as you construct the story of the loss.

Some contractors utilize remote estimators, either in house employees or vendors. A remote estimator can only compose an estimate as good as the details they receive from the field. Whomever completes the onsite walk through must understand the habits for gathering the data in a thorough and consistent manner.

Sketching technologies

Second best is utilizing sketching programs or a good graph notebook. If you are new to sketching for construction estimates, property restoration or Xactimate, we created a video[22] where I teach my young children the basics of measuring and diagraming a room in preparation for an estimate. The video can be found on The DYOJO Youtube page titled *"Improving Your Xactimate Estimates Through Better Claims Sketches."*

If you utilize graph paper, which is the sketching medium that I prefer, the standard format is a square is ¼ inch by ¼ inch and you determine what your scale is. For most claims I prefer ¼ inch equals 2 feet as this allows you to acquire sufficient details and make notations within your sketch. On larger projects

¼ inch may need to equal 5 feet or you may need to acquire a larger pad for big commercial projects.

I still like to do my initial sketches for claims and for asbestos abatement surveys on a sketch pad but have recently updated my platform to an iPad Pro with an Apple Pencil and Goodnotes which allows you to compose on a graph paper background.

I have to admit that I do not have extensive experience with 3D scanning, perhaps the most popular of which is Matterport. This is an emerging technology which will enhance jobsite documentation and may replace the need for traditional sketching. Guests on The DYOJO Podcast, which include Andrew McCabe (Episode 5) and Mark Whatley (Episode 9), have shared their knowledge and Mark's organization Actionable Insights[23] provides training.

The importance of a site visit

One of the most common estimating mistakes includes not conducting a physical site visit to see and feel the extent of the loss for yourself. If you want to achieve the highest compounded value for your estimate, especially on higher value and/or complex losses:

Good documentation from the technicians in the field who completed the mitigation efforts including written notes and photographs of the loss progression.

Utilize technology which includes photographs, 3D scans which allow you to re-walk the loss and scan into details as you structure your estimate and/or take a video walk through of the loss so that you can review for components that you may have forgotten.

Walk the project with the people who are likely to be completing the future work, especially when there are high end details or complexities that make the loss unique.

Have a review process that brings at least one additional set of eyes to review your documentation and estimate structure.

Take pride in what you do. If you are going to be an Xactimate estimator find a way to make your estimates stand out for their clarity and consistent thoroughness.

Whatever you do and how ever you do it, your sketch is key to doing things right, doing them efficiently and providing your client with an excellent representation of the story of their loss. Adding annotations to your sketch can help with communicating the source and extent of the loss.

<u>A few of the key shortcuts available in sketch:</u>

    W – insert a window
    B – square break tool
    M – missing wall
    D – insert a door
    R – insert a room
    SHIFT + W – insert a wall
    C – insert a staircase
    Q – Rotate an Object (great for turning rooms, roofs or staircases).
    "[" & "]" – Using the bracket keys will flip an object, which is great for orienting doors in the proper direction quickly.

Remember, our goal in this book is to help you create the right **mindset** and **habits** to achieve success with developing your career in estimating:

Poorly structured estimates show lack of care and expertise.

This book will help you step your game up or you can throw it in the trash. You can add this book to the myriad of items you blame for your frustrations.

Structural habits will help generate estimating consistency.

Choose either a top-down or bottom-up arrangement. Or keep doing what you've always done. The pros say this is the most effective mantra, right?

Setting your estimate apart from the status quo, in this book we discuss ways to:

Do it right. Do it efficiently. Do it excellently. It sounds too simple to be effective, but I dare you to try it.

Your habits demonstrate your professionalism.

Is it possible to set yourself apart as a contractor, provide value in telling the story of your loss for your customer and communicate effectively with the carrier? No. The answer is no. Stop reading this book, it's just untested drivel by a mediocre author and even worse podcaster.

CHAPTER 6:

Estimating with Xactimate
- Commandment 2

Thou Canst Not Take Too Many Photos.

I can remember when I started in the industry in 2002, the leading technology was the Sony Mavica which captured quality photos onto 3.5 inch floppy disks. Physical job files were weighed down with multiple disks.

The 3.5 inch floppy disk held an average of 1.44 megabytes and according to the internet if you had an average 4x6 photo at about 20-80 KB then your average per floppy disk would be roughly 15 photos, which sounds about right from my recollection.

Even prior to that you would have to take your photos to the print shop to get them processed which was cumbersome. Oftentimes the photos were poor quality or you would lose the key photo that you needed. Today, with digital photos, it is possible to receive documentation from the field in real time.

With the right tools, technicians can even mark up photos

with notes, tags and even measurements. There is no longer an excuse not to have enough photos on any loss.

The more photos that you take the better. Yet, without proper training, you may not receive the photos that you need to help you achieve estimating clarity. Technicians, project managers and estimators need to be trained on how to take photos.

Always take photos of the front of loss, many carriers are re-questing/requiring photos of the rear of the loss as well so why not get a full four corner shot of the exterior of the home?

I am a big fan of consistency so start your photo sequence from the reported source of the loss and then work your way out from there.

Each room should have a photo taken from each of the four corners of the room (assuming that it is a box). Within reason, photos should be taken of every room in the home. It is good practice to document, for potential liability reasons, the condition of the home and all of the items prior to the arrival of your crews. This can also be conducted with a video walkthrough or 3D scan.

All affected building materials and contents should be documented in detail.

Once equipment is set, each piece and a broad view of the equipment in the room should be taken daily, or at least with each re-check of the structure during mitigation.

Whether you are doing content manipulation, a full pack out or simply covering items, it is important to take photos of the items in their prior state. Take pictures of where they were located and then note any prior damages before your team moves them. Many customers may not realize how aged their furniture and items are.

Once you are complete with the repairs and have created a new home for them, their aged furniture and items may stand out and their memories may be hazy with regards to prior conditions. Having time stamped photos showing conditions prior to your team touching those items can be helpful in refreshing their memory.

Every Estimate Needs Two Things

So far our two commandments of Xactimate estimating success have covered two of the most important elements of estimating any project:

The sketch is key to enabling the estimator to efficiently utilize the Xactimate platform.

Photos are essential to justifying your line items, especially where unique or complex elements are involved.

The higher the value and the more complex the process, the more photos need to be taken to support the inevitable questions and/or objections to estimating items that are outside of the norms. Remember, Xactimate is a platform built to capture the most common components of a loss. When the loss you are working on has elements that do not fit in the mold of a "standardized loss", this is when you have to earn your modest salary as an estimator.

Be consistent with your approach

For the common losses, many of which are kitchens and bathrooms on the residential side, learn what carriers and adjusters are looking for. If you don't follow your systems for taking photos the same way each time you visit a loss you will continually waste your time having to run back out to a project just for one shot to justify a key line item. If you live in a high traffic area like I do in Seattle, Washington, that one photo can cost you several hours of productivity.

One of the most common estimating mistakes is not making a physical visit to the site.

If a photo is worth a thousand words...

A 3D scan would be worth ten thousand words (10X)?

Video walkthroughs would be valued similarly to 3D scans - there are advantages and limits to both.

Physical walk throughs have a 40X value as you can take the loss in with all of your senses and get the full 4D experience.

The Funny Thing About Photos (A Rant)

I can remember joining one of the largest restoration firms in the nation and being surprised that their technology was the same, and in some cases less, than the resources we were using when I came into the industry. It is incredible how fast things are changing in general and even faster with technology.

I am not so young that I believe all new tech is the answer but I am not so old that I am tech adverse.

I think technology, as a means of adaptation, must be embraced. But, whatever innovations you embrace should make life better, more efficient or assist you to deliver a higher level of quality. Often, technology can be more cumbersome to utilize than prior methods. This is poor design.

When I arrived at the aforementioned company, they were using busted up cameras that had duct tape on the battery packs and still had a Sony Mavica! It warmed and chilled my heart at the same time. I was nostalgic and yet appalled, wondering how they would even download the pictures. Then I discovered my assigned desktop still had a 3.5" floppy drive.

I had made it to the Emerald City and peered behind the curtain, only to find, like Dorothy, that the Wizard was just a man. Photos were a demand by every estimator and yet no one wanted to invest in updated digital cameras. We couldn't spend $100 to get the gear that our technicians needed to complete their work.

What were the objections when I wanted to buy new gear? "These technicians don't care, they don't take care of anything." Interesting. It's always the front line employees who bear the brunt of the blame rather than digging into the process.

Why do I mention this in a book about estimating? Because, this is Commandment Two, as an estimator you rely on documentation from your team members. If you are too cheap to invest in good equipment, don't have a system that teaches employees how to utilize their tools and don't have a consistent training methodology, you will reap what you sow. It's a self-fulfilling prophecy that technicians don't care when the system doesn't invest in them.

Estimators cannot be silos, you have to participate in building the system that will benefit you directly, attract good people to the team and help your organization gain ground on their goals. Estimators have roles and responsibilities, they are not royalty. I am not a fan of the individuals who believe they are and the systems that promote that ideology.

An estimator needs a brand new F150 with bluetooth and four wheel drive or they throw a fit but the technicians are belittled when their $100 digital camera accidentally fell into a puddle of human waste when they were taking pictures for the estimator in a sewage filled crawl space. Why don't people want to work for $15/hr in property restoration?

An Estimators Gotta Estimate

A few quick tips from David Baker of Home Estimating Services[24]. As of the time of first publication for this book, his team has completed 425 estimates totaling 37 million dollars in property loss valuation for multiple clients:

If you can't build something in your head, how can you build it in Xactimate? Find ways to get some field experience before you write losses.

Don't pretend that you know everything, listen and learn from others daily.

Understand your costs and work up a budget to complete the job before you start the job.

When you price the job you want to live in the world of reality on the high side of fair.

Develop Intentionally From The Start

If you have a growth mindset, you will never be "done" learning or improving in your craft. Estimating is a great challenge and provides a valuable starting point for the valuable services that your organization provides in helping home and business owners restore their property following a damage event.

As David mentions above, and as Kirk mentioned previously, you need to get some hands on experience for how things are constructed and how they go back together. Building something from scratch has it's challenges and rewards. Repairing something something following a water or fire damage has another layer of obstacles and achievements.

One thing that drew me into this industry is that everyday is always something new. Water, fire and smoke all find unique ways to damage a structure. A small occurrence can lead to extensive damages whereas a large event could be contained to a specific area within the structure.

Take your opportunities to get out of the office, to check on the work that is being done, the accuracy of your estimate and the changes in how the industry approaches mitigation as well as repairs. Develop intentionally.

CHAPTER 7:

Estimating with Xactimate
- Commandment 3

Thou Shalt Label Thy Photos Descriptively.

Common descriptions should include the room name and what is being represented with the photograph such as "Kitchen floor damage" or "Living room - ceiling affected". Insurance carriers are often requesting that photos be uploaded in relation to the sequence of rooms in the sketch, this can be easily done by dragging photos into the rooms when uploading into Xactimate.

Photo Names

Make sure the names of the rooms in your sketch are the same names you use to label your photos. Telling the story of the loss means helping those who are reading your estimate to track with your documentation.

Photo Quantities

The number of photos and the depth of the descriptions should be in relationship to the value and complexity of the item you are addressing. A picture is worth a thousand words so utilize this resource to help you communicate the story of the loss and the need for the deviations from the norm that you are requesting.

In The DYOJO Podcast Episode 5[25] we discuss how *innovation is the only way forward* with our guest Andrew McCabe. He shares a few tricks from his years of experience working remotely on claims through his company, Claims Delegates. Listening to this discussion will help property restoration contractors with ideas to help them innovate their way through this pandemic.

We discuss Andy's background in the property restoration industry and his evolution as The Godfather of Remote Estimating. When he took the plunge into being a freelancing remote estimator, this was not a concept that many had heard of, especially in the world of water and fire damage repairs. He shares his experiences with the Matterport 3D scanning camera and how this has helped him to elevate his Xactimate estimating for insurance claims.

As noted previously, the property restoration industry is full of generous entrepreneurs who engage and share their experiences. Remember, most of what your peers know they have had to learn by trial and error. While some make it their mission to police the internet for restoration faux pas, the majority of people I have reached out to have been incredibly helpful. If you need help, ask. If someone reaches out to you for help, remember where you were when you were in their shoes.

Some considerations for those on the fence about 3D scanning for insurance claims:

The details that you can acquire from the field far exceed those available from traditional photos. Not that long ago, Polaroid cameras were all the rage and every file was stacks and stacks of freshly printed hard copies. Or, you had to take your 35mm film to a one hour processing kiosk before you knew whether your photography skills had produced anything useful.

The Sony Mavica floppy disc camera introduced many old dogs to the digital age, but were cumbersome as your data was contained in piles of three and a half inch disks in your file cabinets?

Whether you hire freelance remote estimators or your project managers write Xactimate estimates based upon field documents created by technicians, the 3D scan can expedite their ability to gather the details of the loss. Remember, an accurate sketch is the core of the estimating build out and through photos are the key to capturing, composing and defending line items.

What will you do if you have to defend your documentation in court and you are up against a consultant who uses this technology? Andy McCabe's famous tagline is, "The thickest file wins," and this innovation is going to be utilized by those who want to pick your billing apart.

Mr. McCabe closes his time with us on The DYOJO Podcast (thedyojopodcast.com) with a poignant quote for any entrepreneur and/or small business owner, "The road of life is paved with squirrels who couldn't make a decision." Life is coming at us fast and the market is rapidly changing. We don't know what things will look like year-to-year, but we do know that it will NOT be business as usual.

Treat your photos and your descriptions as though each one were critical to your ability to get paid for the loss. Photo descriptions can be a time-suck but they play a vital role in getting your estimate approved which is key to you being able to secure the contract, so give your photos their due.

If you have a mitigation division and are adept and securing the work for repairs on those projects, set up a process where your technicians are naming the photos as they work through the loss to expedite the backend work for estimators and/or have someone in the office that assists with this process.

Improve profitability by reducing duplication

Reducing unnecessary duplication is one the simplest means to improving efficiency and profitability. Review processes such as photo integration to determine if there are gains you can net by adjusting your process within your team.

"Thickest file wins," is easy to remember and communicates the mindset that will help you develop your habits to achieve your goals. An accurate sketch with annotations that help tell the 2D or 3D story of the loss are the baseline and photos with good descriptions are the foundation for defending a well written estimate.

We have worked with contractors who utilize before and after video walkthroughs of the loss. This can help document the structure in it's damaged condition, including locations for contents, prior to starting work.

When the contractor does a final walkthrough prior to releasing the structure to the client, these videos and/or photos can do wonders for reminding clients, adjusters and carriers how drastic your efforts have been. 3D cameras can play a role in advancing your ability to capture these details before, during and after a project is completed.

When considering new technologies, some helpful questions include:

What is the purpose of the tool and which resource is best suited for that purpose? For example, if your goal is to create before and after video slide shows both for marketing and for providing clients, the quality of the images will be important.

What tools will help expedite existing processes? Many of the professionals that we talked to estimate that the typical 3D camera can be utilized to scan a 1,500 SF house in about an hour. That may be more time that many are used to but does it also provide details that wouldn't otherwise be available?

How can you expedite your ability to safely share photos, videos and/or 3D scans with all stakeholders to allow detailed reviews of the loss site. A whole structure scan eliminates concerns about missing a measurement or not having a key picture needed of the damaged area.

Which tools will allow some efficiency gains, such as training your mitigation team to document and share their findings so that they can reduce the need for additional onsite visits by up-line team members?

If you were taken to court and you had to defend your workmanship, are your documentation processes and resources able to stand up to the scrutiny of a consultant who is using the latest and greatest technology?

Be An Artist

Writing for Restoration & Remediation Magazine (R&R), John Pastrava's article "3 Things Estimators Can Do to Improve Consistency in Their Restoration Estimates[26]" notes:

> *"Creating estimates is an art. Learn your craft, know your craft, and use your craft to the best of your ability. A consistent, well-constructed estimate is like a tightly written, three act screenplay. Its story and content will jump off the pages (or more likely computer screen) in the eyes of any file examiner who reads it and you will be a box office superstar to the policyholders you help rebuild their lives."*

Being an artist is a mindset and developing your ability to craft your masterpiece requires habits. Property restoration estimating is a blend of art and science. You have to know the hard truths of construction and the science of mitigation yet communication is an art form.

Speed is important. The customer wants the job done sooner rather than later. The carrier wants to close the file. If you do program work there are literally ticking clocks and timeline requirement. You know as a business owner or manager that getting in and getting out is critical to being profitable.

While I am not a fan of promoting speed, as focusing on speed alone often leads to sloppiness, pace is an important factor in efficiency. I tried to encourage my teams to focus on **SPEeD** when they would arrive on a new jobsite.

Scan the site to understand the source and extent of the loss.

Plan your strategy for where you will start, how you will address the damages and what your daily production goals are.

Execute your plan. Team members need to communicate with each other and find ways to adapt the plan as they acquire new information.

Document your efforts. As we have said multiple times, we don't get paid for what we do, we get paid for what we document.

These principles apply to estimators as well. When you arrive on the property, scan the loss site so that you have an understanding of the source and extent of the damages. Compose an esitmate that communicates a plan to address the damages. Structure your estimate in a way that it can be utilized as a production plan.

Estimators who understand the production progress can help set their teams ups for success by providing them with the information they need to execute the plan, reduce waste and be efficient in their work. As changes are discovered, be sure that your team understands what and how to document these changes so that you can charge for legitimate supplemental work.

CHAPTER 8:

Estimating with Xactimate
- Commandment 4

Thou Shalt Utilize Thy F9 Notes.

Once you begin estimating in Xactimate, you understand that the platform is rather transparent. An estimate starts with the sketch, and then in each of the affected rooms you insert the line items that are relevant to the details of the particular loss you are working on. These line items add up to form the narrative of the story you are attempting to tell through this medium. Key supplements to the story of the loss include:

Opening statement - this is a great place to present the beginning narrative of the story of the loss. As we will discuss in the next chapter (Commandment V), you can use the 12 hour update for mitigation or the loss narrative for repairs to help create the outline for the content you present.

An accurate sketch with annotations (Commandment I)

Line items with F9 notes (we discuss these in the coming paragraphs)

Photographs which have been labeled descriptively (Commandment III)

To communicate the story of the loss, especially for line items that are outside of the norm, you can add what are called "F9 Notes" to help you convey additional context in support of your estimating approach. These are called F9 notes because you can literally utilize the "F9" button as a shortcut for initiating this resource.

I like to use F9 notes to create an initial structure and/or headings for each room. As noted previously, be consistent with how you approach a claim and be consistent with how you structure your estimates - either top to bottom or bottom to top.

F9 notes can be used for formatting your estimate by breaking up large sections of line items into categories that make the estimate easier to read for reviewers, adjusters and your production teams. Some of the most common headers I use are prep items, walls and ceilings, trim and paint as well as floors and cleaning.

F9 notes can be used to describe how a line item is being utilized, for example DRY LF may have an F9 note of "Repair flood cuts for common wall to bathroom" especially if there is another drywall line item in the room that may be for the ceiling or separate section of wall.

One side note here, when you are repairing flood cuts (typically a 2' high cut in a wall completed during mitigation), DRY

LF will give you more money for these repairs than using DRY ½ as a square footage (SF) total. I'm consistently surprised by how many estimators don't use this simple variance when the line item was clearly developed for this scenario.

DRY LF is the approprite line item for flood cut repairs, but if you stop there then you are leaving legitimate dollars on the table. As a general rule, if you use the DRY LF line item, then you should extend the texture at least an additional 2' beyond all sides of that repaired section. Seal and paint (PNT SP) at least an additional 2' beyond all sides of the texture blend. Once the wall has been repaired, textured, sealed and painted, you want to paint at least the remainder of that surface one coat to blend the repair.

If you decide to utilize a labor (LAB) line item you must understand that it is likely going to be questioned and should have an ample F9 note, photographic support for the scope being requested and best to have the designation as "approved by adjuster," assuming that you have already discussed it with them.

Communication is key to success

The presiding principle of this book should have convinced you that communication is key to successfully navigating the claims process. Your job is to advocate for the insured to help document and propose a plan of action that restores them to pre-loss conditions. No more, no less. F9 notes are a simple, effective and yet under-utilized resource for those who are doing their due diligence to tell the story of the loss.

Communication is a shared responsibility for the key stakeholders in the claims process - the client, the contractor and the carrier. The contractor often has somewhat of the middle ground in applying what the carrier reveals of the content of the policy as applied to the specifics of the loss for the client.

Contractors should be clear about their responsibilities

As we have said before, the goal is to restore the client to pre-loss conditions, no-more and no-less. If the client is trying to game the system to exceed the nature of their policy and the contractor is party to this effort, they are both subject to potential fraud. If the carrier is trying to whittle the claims allocation down to twigs and the contractor plays along, the client is being shorted in effect by collusion.

While it is in the nature of many estimators and contractors to desire to serve their clients best interest, they should be careful to clarify the responsibility of the client rather than to absolve them of any accountability. Often in the sales pitch, contractors tell customers that they will take care of everything, the client will owe nothing and the process will be a breeze. Unfortunately, this creates the wrong expectation.

We want our clients to be invested and engaged in the process. They may need to help us get a response from their insurance carrier, they will need to make timely decisions about materials selections and change orders and they may need to get involved with the process of securing the payment.

What Are Some Of The Common Estimating Issues?

Turn your common estimating issues[27] into training opportunities and achieve long term solutions by sourcing responses to these points of frustration:

Common Issue One

Poor carrier and program basic level compliance.

Response: Clear training and consistent processes for estimate compliance.

Common Issue Two

Poor execution of initial estimate components.

Response: Better attention to details. Learn to become a better claims storyteller.

Common Issue Three

Lack of clarity regarding proper use of line items relevant to the claim.

Response: Skills development through research, peers and training as well as learning from prior rejections.

Common Issue Four

Poor illustrative support for proposed scope of work.

Response: As you develop your story telling abilities, make sure your stories are packed with good pictures.

Common Issue Five

Frustration with the claims review process.

Response: Gather data that will inform decisions so that progress[28] can be made.

CHAPTER 9:

Estimating with Xactimate
- Commandment 5

Thou Shalt Document Thy Initial Findings.

I opened the book with my initial career aspirations to be involved in forensics. In many ways, our initial approach to a loss should resemble that of the arrival of crime scene investigators to an active crime scene. Especially when there has been a fire, you want to cordon off the source area to ensure the local fire investigator as well as the carrier's independent forensic consultant have "cleared the scene".

The fire department representative is primarily concerned with whether a potential crime has been committed whereas the forensic investigator that a carrier will send is looking to determine if there are any grounds from subrogation. If the insurance company can find a means of compensation from another entity, they will pursue it.

In a water damage situation, we typically start from the source of the loss and work our way out. In a fire damage situation, the source area needs to be kept in its current conditions until the process can be completed.

I can remember being scolded rather handily for working in the source area first on a small residential fire. When the forensic investigator from the insurance carrier arrived I was grilled on why I had touched the room and the appliance suspected of being the point of origin and for turning the power off at the electrical panel. Stumbling, I told this person that I was doing what I was told and that the fire department had "released the scene." He did not like that answer. "No one releases the scene but me!"

This professional thought themselves to be rather important but I learned an important lesson from the experience. If you are in a position of leadership, don't assume your team members just know the drill. You need to train regularly for various scenarios, communicate work scopes unique to each project and use errors as an opportunity to train the team.

Secure the scene

When you arrive, treat the loss as a crime scene of sorts. Start your process with detailed documentation of the structure, contents and damages in a thorough and consistent manner. Use photos, video, audio and notes to capture the details of the loss at each stage.

If you are dealing with contents, whether it's just moving a single refrigerator or packing out an entire home, capturing the conditions of these items prior to touching them is critical. You may notice that there are scratches, scrapes and leftover food plastered on the stainless steel refrigerator, these items may become a point of contention when you bring the unit back into the kitchen following the completion of your work.

Whether a client is an opportunist, just waiting for you to mess up in the slightest way, or has as foggy of a memory as the rest of us, if you made the customer aware prior to moving the item and took a photo of the pre-existing damages, you will be in better standing that trying to defend yourself without this evidence.

Following your first walk through on a new project, you should develop a habit for documenting your initial findings. Whether it's a 12 hour update for a mitigation claim or a loss narrative for a repairs claim, you need to communicate the conditions you have found once you have completed your this inspection. These should be sent as emails as soon as possible following the outset of the project and followed up by a phone call (or vice versa).

For mitigation projects you are communicating the site conditions, source and drying plan.

For repairs projects you are confirming the site conditions and outlining the scope of work that you are estimating for.

Samples of what should be covered in the twelve hour update for a mitigation project should include the following information sent to inform the carrier.

12 hour update for mitigation

Was extraction performed

Source of loss (communicate category and class of water)

Rooms affected (it helps to provide a general scope of mitigation)

Initial moisture readings

Equipment set (this is a good time to request approval for any specialty equipment)

Estimated duration of drying (you may need to request more than 3 days of drying time, document why.

Any lead, asbestos or other conditions that may delay mitigation

On the repair side, we often call this initial update a loss narrative which includes the information a carrier needs to prepare for the nature of the claim.

Loss narrative for repairs

Source of loss

Condition of home

General scope (it helps to provide a general breakdown by room/area)

Any specialty conditions

Mastery of Xactimate, and anything else for that matter, comes through the ability to do it right, then do it efficiently and finally to discover ways to do it excellently.

Do it right.

I believe mastery is a process of first, doing it right. If you cannot do it right, you cannot achieve mastery. First and foremost, your responsibility is to learn to use the tool of Xactimate to correctly communicate the scope of work that will be necessary to return the structure of your client to pre-loss conditions.

Many people have some strong opinions about what is right, and hopefully you will form your own opinions after learning to use the tool correctly.

Doing it right with Xactimate includes:

Using the right line items for the scope of work

Supporting your estimate items with F9 notes and photos

Learning from your mistakes

Do it efficiently.

Once you have learned the basics and you know how to use the tool correctly - once you can do it right - then you must learn to be efficient. I try very hard to only tell people to do something faster if that is literally the only thing I need them to focus on. When you tell someone to work faster, it usually results in throwing out the first principle of doing it right. Faster leads to shortcuts. What we want to teach our team members to think about is how to be more efficient.

We discuss this principle of efficient vs. fast in The DYOJO Podcast Episode 18, which is also Pro vs. Joe 003[29]. Our Pro vs. Joe Podcast[30] within a podcast is a fun exercise where myself and Bryan Close discuss learning the industry from two unique perspectives.

It has been a fun process for me as it forces me to talk through many of the things we take for granted when we have been in the industry for some time as well as the opportunity to see property restoration again through fresh eyes.

Efficiency in estimating includes things like first knowing your line items and then memorizing those ones that you use most frequently. This helps you to write quicker but also helps you understand the structure of Xactimate so that you have a better idea of how to find non-typical line items.

Efficiency as an organization means finding tools, resources and processes that help you to capture details, share them with all parties, reduce redundancy and more rapidly export estimates so that you can keep your teams working.

Doing it efficiently with Xactimate includes:

Memorizing the line item codes

Using a consistent structure for your estimate

Creating a process for gathering data, composing solid estimates and conducting an internal review

Do it excellently.

Finally, when you know how to do it right and you are operating efficiently, then you want to add a flair of excellence. We want this for our mitigation and repair teams, as this is what leads to repeat customers. We want our clients bragging on how well our teams do their jobs and achieving that starts with training everyone to do their job right, to do their job efficiently and to find ways to do their job excellently.

In estimating, I believe it is both efficient and excellent to set up a consistent structure for your estimates. Adjusters, reviewers and claims professionals should look at your estimate and recognize the structure. How many estimates have you seen where the line items are just thrown at the wall with no thought as to their relevance nor any structure to their placement in the sequence of the loss.

When you establish a structure, it helps you as the estimator to capture details consistently, to compose them in a way that reminds you not to miss items and enables whomever is reviewing your estimate to track along with the flow of your estimate to expedite their response.

If you need your team working so that you are bringing revenue in, you need estimates going out the door. If you need profitable jobs to be wrapping up on a consistent basis so that you can pay your people, your bills and keep your operation growing, you need estimates going out the door.

As I said, it's not just sending out estimates faster, but finding a way to send good estimates (written accurately), exported consistently and efficiently so that they can be translated into profitable work. Structure your system to optimize this flow.

Doing it excellently with Xactimate includes:

Finding a way to make your estimates stand out from your competitors

Structuring your estimates in a way that expedites review, approval and the transition into production

Take note that the process of mastery requires a commitment to these three principles of doing it right, doing it efficiently and doing it excellently. If you lead by example in this process you can inspire others while you explore ways to incorporate this process into everything that you do in your organization.

The Four P's Of The Blueprint For Success[31]

P1 is for People

When it is difficult to find people at all, growth minded businesses understand the value of investing in developing internal talent. Investing in the employees you have can produce significant returns on your investment (ROI).

P2 is for Process

It is important for leaders to review whether their processes are in alignment with their vision. If there are setbacks to growth, a good place to start would be in reviewing the processes that are in place.

P3 is for Production

Production issues help to reveal shortcomings in processes.

Often failure helps us to better see areas we can improve than success does. Be sure to embrace the opportunity to grow as a leader and a team.

P4 is for Progress

Like a flourishing garden, growth in an organization is attractive and creates a sense of pride. If we invest in our people, process and production then we will find that progress is much more attainable.

CHAPTER 10:

Estimating with Xactimate
- Commandment 6

Thou Shalt Update Thy Adjuster In Real Time And Document Consistently.

T he foundation for success in any organization, as well as the development of your project management system, is communication. Property restoration requires technical knowledge in the multiple service disciplines as well as the ability to communicate these details across several data entry points to keep the various stakeholders updated on the progress of a given loss.

Then you multiply that process by how heavy your workload is and you have many opportunities for details to be missed, updates to lag and the customer experience to falter.

Communication is a core issue

If you are struggling to provide your clients and claims stakeholders with consistent updates on production, this is usually an indication that there are greater issues within your process. We discuss in our article, *Garbage In, Garbage Out*[32], how this can often be traced back as far as how we answer the call when a new loss or project comes into our office.

If we are not consistent in how we gather details, share that information and prepare our teams for responding, these inconsistencies will carry through all of our processes.

Do we have a consistent process for gathering as much information as we can when a call for service comes in? Regardless of who answers the phone, we should have a clear and consistent process for acquiring the details necessary to set our teams up for success.

When we answer the phone, we communicate to our customers that we care by getting the details right and we communicate to our service employees that we care by providing them with the details they need to start a project off with good information.

This is important both for your front line technicians responding to calls for new losses as well as your estimators who are scheduling their days to meet their current project load as well as the incoming workflow.

Clarity At The Point of Work Initiation

Disaster response means that work comes in at all hours of the day as pipes break, fires occur or a host of other scenarios play out for homes and businesses in your market. Because of these contingencies, our schedules can never be fixed to the point that they have no flux in them but we should be working to be *the calm in the chaos*[33] both when we meet with customers as well as in our internal operations.

Our people deserve to know, as best as management is able to communicate, what their assignment will be for the following 24 hour period so that they can mentally prepare and ready their teams to respond to our customers needs.

Our customers deserve to have consistent communication of job progress and to know when strangers are going to be in their home.

Clarity and consistency in communication requires the commitment of everyone in the organization, top to bottom - from the point of receiving a call for service to the completion of a project. We have to be intentional about improving our systems as the systems (good or bad) do not create themselves. Our systems may never be perfect, but we will reap what we sow.

If the phone rings more often than it should with confused or upset customers, follow the layers to yourself and get to work on fixing the problems with the system.

Follow the Rule of No Surprises

A key principle I learned early on from Denis Beaulieu (our guest on The DYOJO Podcast Episode 15[34]) was, "No surprises." This is something I have tried to carry through all of my teams as I trained them to respond to our clients needs. Denis asked that he never be surprised by something that happened at a customer's home or business.

The principle being that if you mess up and you tell me about it, we can work together to find a solution. But if the customer discovers it and the manager finds out about it via an angry call from the homeowner, then our opportunity to get ahead of the issue has been lost. Rather than winning the client over by being proactive together we are now in damage control.

One time we received a call from a homeowner asking where their lamp was. They noted, it wasn't anything special but it was missing. I don't recall when we discovered it's whereabouts but the lamp was broken and behind the couch. A sub contractor probably bumped it by accident and rather than make us aware so that we could purchase another one and have the replacement ready for the client, we had egg on our face for breaking and then hiding the evidence.

I used this as a great opportunity to discuss again with our team the importance of "no surprises". The lamp was less than twenty dollars at Walmart and the customer had a good laugh about the ordeal. Thankfully the project was completed shortly after otherwise this could have impacted their willingness to trust our team and our subs in their home.

Most clients don't expect us to never make a mistake, but how you respond to errors says a lot about your organization. This is true with your customers as well as with your team. If you are defensive with clients when you are in the wrong, you will struggle to build trust. If you overreact with employees, you will struggle to build trust.

Denis also sums this up in something he learned from one of his managers, "Everything you tell a customer before you begin is information. Everything after is generally an excuse[35]."

He explains the story behind this quote, "I was told this many years ago when we had performed an abatement project that went wrong. Simply the estimator didn't let the owner know we were going to be blocking off the areas and they wouldn't have access. Didn't tell them about containment damages, didn't mention having to turn the water off if the valves leaked and that they could possibly have no water.

So, after the fact I had to explain that this was all in the contract but they're complaint was they were never told and had to leave and get a hotel on short notice. My regional told me that everything the estimator told her before we started was information, or lack of, and after we were done was just excuses."

Use the tools at your disposal

Utilize email, text, phone calls and third-party programs such as Xactanalysis to communicate consistently and clearly with all parties. While some adjusters may have you wait until the end of a claim to compose all of your supplements and changes, you want to make sure that you aren't waiting until then to communicate and acquire some form of written approval.

You want to build relationships with adjusters and claims administrators and communication is a means to making their job easier by not surprising them with alterations to the plans previously agreed to.

When something is out of the ordinary, make a phone call and discuss it with the assigned adjuster as soon as possible.

Follow up all phone conversations with an email requesting affirmation of the items discussed and/or agreed to.

Track all changes, even if they are zero dollar changes, so that you can show that you are attempting to create a transparent and fair process.

In so far as you are able, keep the process peaceful. Try to give people the benefit of the doubt when you are unsure if they are doing something that you perceive to be wrong or hurtful.

When you are met with opposition, ask questions. If an adjuster cannot approve a line item, ask if there is another way that you can approach the scope of work. Remember, everyone has a boss and if someone is going to travel down the path of the unusual with you, supply them with the information they need to justify the variance.

On Episode 6[36] of The DYOJO Podcast, Raymond Tittmann, of Tittmann Weix, shared his thoughts and advice for property restoration contractors who were responding to COVID-19 related cleaning services. The advice he gives applies to all levels of service and response with regards to setting your process up for success when working with insurance carriers:

Communication: Response without any prior communication to the insurance company creates issues in the carrier, client and contractor paradigm. Whether intentionally or not, this can create problems with confirming coverage which will impact the process for all parties involved.

Documentation: All business owners and cleaning contractors should do their due diligence to create a "fair record" that there was contamination present in the space so that the insurance companies can determine exposure and support a legitimate response to the issues affecting the client.

Provide Value: Whenever services are offered, the contractor should be able to document that value was provided to the client and be able to relay the story of the loss to the insurance company who is adjusting the claim.

CHAPTER 11:

Estimating with Xactimate
- Commandment 7

Thou Shalt Learn Thy Carrier's Guidelines

While it is impossible to remember all of the sundry carrier guidelines, unless you are able to specialize with specific carriers, it is important to know the most commonly rejected line items. Pay attention to what you are getting rejected for. Try to not repeat the same mistakes with the same carriers.

Every carrier has their general rules as well as their idiosyncrasies. For example, as previously mentioned, one carrier will want content manipulation written out as CON LAB and another will want to see it as CON ROOM. It should only take one rejection for you to understand and remember which carrier prefers the line item one way or the other.

Low hanging fruit

One approach to estimating, especially if you work with a carrier that has rigorous reviews, is to present what I like to call "low hanging fruit". By nature of the process, the adjuster or reviewer has to reject (adjust) something or are they doing their job? In this mindset, if the carrier has to reject something to feel good about the process, then give them some easy things to review, reject and cut from your estimates.

Review your rejections

What you should also understand about the review process is that when they take a microscopic look at your estimate and reject items, this presents you with an opportunity to re-review your own estimate.

If you are sending back an estimate with revised line items you had better have found a few new things to throw at them for review as well. There is a strong likelihood that you missed a few legitimate things the first time around, add those into your estimate before you send the revised version.

Naming conventions

When you compose an estimate, always write your first draft the way that you would approach the claim. Even if you suspect this will never get accepted, create the estimate and save it. If you don't already have a naming convention, my preference is:

YRMO_LAST_F-Revision

For example, an estimate written in May of 2005 for David Smith would be 0505_SMIT_D. If you write a revised version then that would be saved as 0505_SMIT_D-1

Play the game with class and sass

Many estimators view the review and rejection process as a moral assault on their abilities as professionals. This is a mindset that will most certainly lead you to burnout. The right mindset is to view the review as part of the process, or a component of "the game".

Our job, then, is to know the rules of this game and to find ways to excel within those boundaries. You can have sass, but do it with class. Also, don't beat yourself up over trying to compose the perfect estimate, I doubt such a thing exists given that the metrics are judged and interpreted by other humans.

Focus on consistently gathering thorough details and composing an accurate estimate while mastering the tools at your disposal to communicate the story of the loss.

Quantity over quality?

Unfortunately, many companies set an unrealistic standard of trying to get as few rejections as possible. These organizations are solely playing the numbers, and believe that quantity is better than quality. It's a strategy that has worked for many successful companies in other industries. It can be a miserable living in the property restoration world.

Most estimators know how to get their estimates approved, but I question how much fat you can trim before you start cutting into meat and eventually hitting bone. It's nice to have a ribeye steak with the bone in, but it's another thing to be constantly served bone soup when you were promised a meat buffet.

If your system is designed around maintaining a low rejection rate at any cost, your margin expectations should reflect the rejection strategy. Turn and burn will be your pathway to fighting for success. Managers and business owners who are reading this book should take note that estimators should not be penalized for margin shortfalls in a process that all but guarantees them.

Are you trying hard enough?

Another way to look at this process is, if you aren't getting rejected then you aren't trying hard enough. This is not to say that you should find ways to work around the system, but you should find ways to use the system to push at the boundaries. As such, knowing what is and isn't included in a line item is a key resource for being able to use Xactimate to tell the story of the loss, advocate for your strategy and defend your estimate.

As we will discuss in the chapter titled, *Help! Claims Review Shredded My Estimate*[37], there is plenty about the estimating process that can leave a professional frustrated. Don't forget to take a breather, step away from the computer from time to time, and come back at your estimate with a fresh set of eyes. Property restoration has plenty of opportunities, even if you are working for a company that does program work, the game can be enjoyable.

Xactiamte Master Class

Ben Justesen, President of Enlightened Restoration Solutions[38], shares a portion of his Xactimate mastery journey:

"I believe that if one is to be successful they have to go

down the difficult path. When I committed to estimating, my first week doing it I went to a class in Utah at Xactware to be trained formally. From polling people that come to my classes, I would say that 90% of estimators do not get formal training which I believe is crucial for any estimator to start and be more successful."

Focusing On The Right Things

Regardless of the industry that you are in, you are in a fight for survival. Too often we make things more complicated than they need to be and we ask peopel in our organizations to focus on things that are outside of their control.

For those that do not understand what it takes to start, maintain and grow a business, you have to be profitable. In short, you must earn more than you spend. Similar to the recipe for success with your personal finances, the business must have a vision, live on budget and make smart choices with it's money.

I believe you need two things to remain in business, you need to be profitable (make money) and you need to have happy customers. While many don't understand what it truly means to make money, you must understand that just because your company charges $20,000.00 for a project that does not mean they are making, or keeping, $20,000.00 for the company or for the owners.

We go into greater details on job costs and how the estimator must understand these in Chapter 13. All employees can grasp how they play a role in helping the company to be profitable and to make customers happy. I would argue that the second is the more important one.

When you teach your people how to master the customer

experience, you have a much greater chance of achieving a positive customer experience that will lead to better long term referrals, a better reputation and some mercy when your team makes a mistake.

Your team members can get behind a vision that is centerend around them taking care of the customer more readily than one that is based in making the most money possible. A customer centered value system leads to less confusion over what should be done when there is a problem and leads to less temptation to cut corners when things get tight.

In short, focusing on the numbers as an end in themselves rarely leads to a positive outcome with regards to customer experience, employee engagement and overall achievement of organizational goals.

This does not mean that the numbers don't matter, it means that they should be understood, taught and communicated in the context of the overall vision and value the company brings to the market.

If you focus on making money, you will struggle to achive happy customers as they are lost in the numbers. Conversely, if you focus on the customer experience, you will find ways to become profitable while also increasing your legacy.

You may not agree with me, and that is fine. But, are the things that you are focusing on leading to the outcomes that you want to achieve? Or, like many organizations, have you said one thing but promoted another by your mindset and habits such that you are trending in the wrong direction to remain viable in your market?

CHAPTER 12:

Estimating with Xactimate
- Commandment 8

Thou Shalt Know Thy Line Items (Apply Thyself To Understand The Process Of Line Item Approvals).

I f you do not want to be constantly frustrated by rejections you must quickly learn which line items will get rejected by reviewers or will require adjuster approval. When working with third party administrators (TPAs) you will have to work through layers of review and approvals based upon insurance carrier guidelines.

If you have a scope of work that falls outside of the norm you will need to get in communication with the adjuster to discuss how they would like that scope of work broken down. All scope and line items that may not pass through the normal review process can be overridden if there is ample explanation through F9 notes, photos and the designation that this has been "approved by adjuster".

If you engage in marketing to local insurance agents, one value you can offer is providing a free inspection for a potential damage. As you know, sometimes a loss can seem much larger than it is and conversely what seemed like a big problem may not have actually spread that far. In an age when client deductibles are on the rise, a pre-claim inspection can help the agent and client make an informed decision.

For example, if they have a $1,000.00 deductible and you believe the mitigation and repairs will be $1,500.00, you could save everyone on their long term claims history by working with the home or business owner directly. Communicating with the local insurance agent is a great way to provide value to them.

If you arrive at a loss and have not been referred, it is good practice to ask who their local agent is and use the experience as an opportunity to earn their trust and business. The best agents understand that they are paid to be a part of the process and help their clients through these experiences.

Don't mistake the agent for the adjuster. The agent has a responsibility to assist their client with the claims process but they don't have authority when it comes to adjusting the claim. Contacting the agent is a good sales-through-service opportunity and they should be able to help you acquire the contact information for the claims representative.

Agents can and should advocate for their clients but they typically don't have the authority to make decisions regarding the claim. The client should also be involved in the process of contacting both their agent and their adjuster to ensure that they are advocating for themselves. The goal is to restore the home or business to pre-loss conditions. When the client, agent, adjuster and contractor are on the same page, this can help to expedite the process.

Unleash the power of memorization

This is not a commandment but it certainly is helpful - **Thou shalt memorize thy most commonly used line items.** Within six months to a year of writing Xactimate estimates you should be able to call out the line items and write your most frequent estimate scopes without the search function.

The last thing you want to do as an estimator is to leave legitimate money on the table, for your client and yourself as the contractor, when you have a legitimate opportunity to capture and communicate line items that are warranted within the scope of the loss.

A good friend of mine, someone who learned to be proficient in Xactimate in a short amount of time (because they had a mediocre mentor), recently aced a job interview because of memorization. The employer asked him to demonstrate his estimating skills with a piece of paper and a pencil. Because we had worked from the beginning to memorize common line items, this Xactimate blue belt was able to crank out a basic estimate line-by-line from memory.

Having a growth mindset and developing your habits will help you improve your day to day success and could lead to your next great opportunity.

Macros

Many experienced restoration professionals utilize macros for their scopes of work to help them consistently load key line items, as well as those secondary items, that transform an estimate from a shot in the dark into a realistic plan that will make you money.

Your client deserves an estimator who can communicate the scope of the loss in the tool that is understood by the carrier. Macros can be time consuming to set up and edit.

Cut and Paste

Another option is to save and label estimates with key recurring scopes that have been approved as groups for future reference. This may be something like "Bathroom - Toilet Overflow - Insurance X", so that you can use this prior scope to cut and paste and thereby expedite your process moving forward.

As I mentioned previoulsy, I learned Xactimate by copying my manager's estimates and breaking down how he composed his proposals. Imitation is flaterry and it is also a pathway to unlocking your career development in property restoration.

Build your system to your vision

However you approach estimating, you need a consistent system for capturing the details and composing the correct line items to tell the story of the loss. Memorization will help you increase your estimating speed and when combined with a clear structure you will prevent scope creep at the outset of the project.

You should always have your eyes and ears open to improve your process. From time to time you should review an estiamte from another estimator in your office and compare notes on how you both structure your scopess. Whether its learning how someone approached a particular trade or their methods for getting unique items approved with a particular carrier, learn from others.

What is scope creep?

According to Wikipedia[39], "Scope creep (also called requirement creep, or kitchen sink syndrome) in project management refers to changes, continuous or uncontrolled growth in a project's scope, at any point after the project begins. This can occur when the scope of a project is not properly defined, documented, or controlled."

Scope creep starts with failure to capture the details of the loss and composing an accurate estimate. An estimate written with scope creep embedded in the details of the manuscript will start a snowball effect that will plague the rest of the process. Loss of profitability starts with estimating. A poorly written estimate is missing line items, therefore project details and work sequences, which creates an ongoing struggle to gain ground lost from the outset of the project.

Preventing scope creep

Write an accurate and thorough estimate, do you best to capture everything that needs to be done on the project so that you set your team up for success in production and your organization on the path to progress in their profitability goals. The majority of scope creep is preventable.

Please know that I am very familiar with the struggles inherent with program work. What I would often do was sit down for my first draft estimate and compose a proposal based upon how we would approach the project if no TPA or carrier requirements existed. I would save this as the original draft. Then I would go back through and write an estimate based upon what I thought the carrier would approve and save this as revision one (R1).

My goal would be to work my way back to the first draft estimate. I think doing this helps you not to lose your perspective of how things should be when you are too deep in the way things are. When estimate items are removed or revised at the request of the adjuster or reviewer, it is important to document these changes.

Compose Your Estimate In A Manner That It Can Be Utilized By Production.

Structure

When you utilize a top-down or bottom-up structure every time, all parties that review your estimates will be able to track with your estimate flow. Remember, you are telling the story of the loss and stories have structure. When you production team understands your structure it will help them translate the estimate into a project management tool as well.

F9 notes

Utilize your F9 notes to defend you requests for consideration of items outside of the normal scope of Xactiamte and as legends for your production team to understand how you envision the project execution. We spend so much time and energy in creating estimates, if estimators will take a few minutes to think through how the work will be produced, they can optimize their estimate to transition smoothly into the production process.

Labor and materials

While the Xactimate tools aren't 100% accurate, they do help you to set up a budget for material quantities and estimated hours. Use the tool to its full potential including the scope print out which creates a checklist for production out of your line items.

Production plan

Through Xactimate you can print a copy of your estimate as a production plan that displays your line items, F9 notes, square footages and assigns check boxes to each. For budgeting purposes you can also print out labor and materials breakdowns. These shouldn't be relied upon but are a good starting point.

Change orders

Clarify the change order process with your client, the carrier and your production team.

In cases where you know legitimate scope items have been removed from your estimate, make sure the carrier, the client and your production team know that you plan to supplement for these items. Have the discussion with your project manager that you need to document the need, the work and the progress of those key items.

Estimators need to discuss and educate their team members on how they compose estimates so that they know how to produce the work and are empowered to assist with capturing potentially lost scope. Many good carpenters and technicians will complete work because they are doing what they know is right but aren't trained to identify and communicate these add on services so that they can be accurately billed for.

Clarifying what is included in your estimate and what would be supplemental is an important way of preventing scope creep during the process. If you don't capture the details until after the additional work is completed, you will have issues acquiring compensation for these supplements.

Train (your team) to obtain (your goals).

On Episode 17 of The DYOJO Podcast, Eric "The Tech Whisperer" Sprague, talks about the importance of training for employee engagement, company branding and profitability. Conducting regular training will assist you and your team in gaining clarity, consistency and accountability for the items that are important to the long term health of your organization.

Think through your process and ensure that you are providing your team with the information and tools that they need to succeed. The worst thing you can do is assume that your team members know how to do things the right way and that they will understand how to excute your company vision without consistent training.

CHAPTER 13:

Estimating with Xactimate
- Commandment 9

Thou Shalt Know Thy Line Items (Thou Shalt Understand Thy Line Item Descriptions).

When you start writing estimates in Xactimate you need to take some time to familiarize yourself with what is and isn't included in a line item. As a general rule, most carriers do not want you to utilize labor (LAB) line items as in theory everything that needs to be done should be covered in the details of the Xactimate selection.

For those items that are out of the ordinary or uncommon, first ensure that there isn't an Xactimate line item that covers the work you are attempting to utilize a labor line item for. It may take a sequence of searches and reading through descriptions before you find what you are looking for. Or there may be similar line items that you can utilize which will get you closer to the work sequence you are composing and thereby reducing the reliance on purely labor line items.

Prior to using a labor line item, you will want to read the line item description to ensure that you aren't duplicating an aspect of the work that is already covered within the line item(s). Doing your research and applying yourself to this ongoing process is part of a long term strategy for success in estimating, regardless of the platform.

Sloppy estimators throw everything at the wall and hope that it sticks.

Internal reviews before external rejections

If you do not have a consistent system for reviewing your estimating process, refreshing your knowledge of updates to the system and having someone check your estimates, you are cutting yourself short. Knowing the line items helps you to capture elements missing in line items that may be omitted in the description.

There are organizations, such as those we have mentioned in this book, that provide good resources to keep estimators up to date with Xactimate price list changes from month-to-month.

From estimate to production

Knowing your line items, understanding how your team will perform the work and composing your estimate in a consistent structure help to expedite the process from estimating to production. Project management follows estimating and each estimator should understand how their estimate plays a role in the entire process.

How many estimators do not understand their true costs for common items such as labor, burden, materials, equipment, overhead and profit?

What if you wrote to paint all walls and ceilings but the adjuster only approved the wall with the damages? Do you document this with an F9 note and make sure that your client, project manager and production team knows that as well?

If you don't communicate this "cut" from the carrier to the client, what happens when they notice your team only painted one wall and it doesn't match up to the other walls in the room? In an article I published in R&R on leadership quotes, Denis Beaulieu shared one that has stuck with him, "Everything you say before the job starts is an explanation, everything you say after it starts in an excuse." You can save yourself a lot of trouble by communicating with your clients and documenting variances in scope between when you believe is right and what the carrier has ommitted.

How much do you give away in your profitability if your team purchases materials and expends the labor to paint three walls and a ceiling that were not included in the approved scope of work? If this is happening on multiple projects, all for lack of scope clarifitcation, how much is that costing over the course of a month, a quarter or even a year?

Clarity in communication and consistency in your processes will make you money.

Labor costs

Just because Xactiamte pays $X.XX for a trade does not mean that this is accurate for your area. You need to know your labor costs and be ready to support a request for consideration of elevating that line item for labor based upon the unique nature of your local market.

Restoration Industry Association (RIA) has been doing a lot of work in this area recently through their Advocacy and Government Affairs Committee (AGA). If you haven't already seen it, look up the video with Ed "The Restoration Lawyer" Cross and Bill Loveland, one of the founders of Xactware, as they discuss Xactimate pricing.

A brief note on professionalization

Many in the industry have been talking for some time about strategies to formalize the property restoration industry in the model of professional plumbers and electricians. These professions have benefited from a standardized process for apprenticeship and journeyman programs which combine training with field experience which has translated to being able to charge higher rates for the value they provide.

While property restoration has come a long way towards being recognized as a respected profession, thanks to the vision and passion of early innovators like Marty L. King. I wrote about some of these early efforts in an article for Restoration and Remediation Magazine (R&R) titled, "A History of Collaboration, A Future of Advocacy[40]".

In the early 1990's, due to emerging environmental issues surrounding water loss and the need to develop standards for the industry, many members weren't sure if the RIA (then operating as ASCR) was the right vehicle for achieving this goal. Thankfully in 1995 the ASCR leadership called upon Mr. Cliff "The Z Man" Zlotnik to lead a steering group to address water damage specific issues. An industry that was being established by fiercely independent and passionately driven professionals was also embracing the power of collaboration.

1970's - Similar efforts had been made by Marty King who initiated the National Institute of Fire Restoration (NIFR) to bolster the fire restoration operating division within the AIDS banner (the unfortunate name of RIA at the time). When asked what his purpose was when he founded the NIFR, he replied, "My goal was to see the practice of insurance damage repair become a profession."

1990's - NIFR changed its name to the National Institute of Disaster Restoration (NIDR) which was eventually folded into the Disaster Restoration Division of the ASCR.

1995 - Cliff and the water damage committee, developed the Water Loss Institute (WLI) which provided ASCR with two thriving advanced trade designations to assist restorers with specialized education and hands-on training for both water and fire damage response.

1999 - The IICRC, Institute of Inspection Cleaning and Restoration Certification, was hard at work to produce its second edition of the S500 Standard and Reference Guide for Professional Water Damage Restoration (the first edition was released in 1994) but would not release the S520 which would be specific to mold remediation until 2003.

2006 - IICRC S500 (3rd edition) becomes ANSI certified.

While these industry designations have helped to form a more consistent approach to damage response and repairs, they have not yet led to consistent compensatory recognition for employees or the industry. Sending someone to a three day class and passing a test cannot be the only justification for higher rates.

Members of the industry have a responsibility to ensure we are providing a high level of technical service as well as exploring means to quantify this in real value provided to the clients and the carriers.

Labor Burden

Just because your company pays a technician $X.XX per hour does not mean that you add your markup to that and call it good. Labor burden includes additional costs on labor such as payroll taxes, retirement benefits, health benefits, worker's compensation, life insurance, pensions and other fringe benefits. Your true labor costs include the hourly wage plus burden prior to adding overhead and profit.

Burden would include your goals for salary increases, commissions and bonuses. Many new entrepreneurs believe that if they were making $25 an hour at their former job but are now paying themselves $40 an hour, they have made the big times. What entrepreneurs, estimators, manages and technicians fail to understand is that there are many costs that are tacked onto labor which an organization must pay.

If you are an entrepreneur you need to set aside money for costs such as taxes, overhead costs, repairs, retirement, etc. As an estimator you need to understand what your company's labor burden is and factor this into your budget and overall costs. Those indirect costs will add up and can suck out any profitability you have if you are not tracking them correctly.

Materials

As with labor above, you need to understand the cost of materials in your market. The extreme example would be remote areas of Alaska where materials can only be delivered once a day by ferry or via plane. Your cost of materials will be exponentially higher and you have to be ready to communicate and advocate for that before you start the project.

In a scenario where labor and materials have to be transported by ferry to a location, which is common in the Seattle / Tacoma area, you want to account for those additional labor, fees and costs. You can either estimate those costs on the front end or at minimum present your capture plan and get approval in writing from the adjuster.

For example we have used a spreadsheet to capture the daily time and fees and attached that to our estimate as a custom line item. Labor would include average time in line on both sides of the journey, average time in transport and applicable fees. Tally the daily totals and add the markup and then embed in your estimate with an F9 note. Be sure that you discuss and get a documented agreement with the adjuster prior to the start of the project.

Equipment

Understand your equipment costs and/or rental. Make sure that for customized equipment you have accounted for the loading, transport, set up, compliance, training, takedown, transport and unloading. On the mitigation side the carriers and reviewers will require documentation of what kinds of equipment you used, where you placed the equipment and usually have some internal calculator for these items.

If you are writing for water damage mitigation, It will be important to have your documentation in order to justify what you used, why you used it and how well you tracked the data to demonstrate whether your strategy was working. Water damage is an area where the carriers have done the book work and can often speak the language of the IICRC S500 which will keep you on your toes.

Overhead and Profit

I don't want to assume that you know what overhead and profit are. As an introduction, you need to understand that labor, materials and equipment are typically considered direct costs. The labor, materials and equipment that you use for a specific job, should be accounted for by the budget of that job which flows from the estimate created for the scope of work to be performed.

If an estimator bid a project for $10,000.00, excluding taxes and/or fees, lets say the labor is 40% of that total or $4,000.00, the materials are 30% for $3,000.00 and the equipment is $500.00, our direct cost total would be $7,500.00 or 75%. This means we have $2,500.00 or 25% gross profit.

It seems like we pulled off a good project right?

If your company has an operating overhead of 30% and a net margin goal of 10% then you are 15% off the mark. You made money but you didn't hit the goals. You are actually 5% in the hole (simple math) for your overhead costs and another 10% in the hole from the company's projections for the annual average.

This is similar to what new entrepreneurs go through, they are "making money" but they aren't seeing the whole picture. Ben Justesen, who is also from my old stomping grounds in Eastern Washington, that infamous desert oasis known as Moses Lake, does a good job of breaking this down in Episode 27 of The GMS Podcast with Gerrett Stier.

If you want to be profitable, you need to understand all of the factors. On the project listed above, how do you fix the delta? On the estimating side you either needed to charge more for the initial estimate or perhaps you missed some change orders for legitimate additional work. On the project management side you need to find ways to be more efficient with your labor, this could include less wasted time by having materials at the job or clarifying the scope of work before the production team arrives.

Whether you want to get into estimating, working to improve your abilities or training others to develop their skills, it is essential to know the factors for the organization you are working with. You likely won't hit the target on every job, but you need to know what you are aiming for so you can keep yourself making progress towards the goal.

So many contractors want to complain about the 10 & 10 that has become the commonly allowed overhead and profit margin. If you are not aware, the insurance industry has perpetuated an expectation that restoration contractors do fine on 10% overhead and 10% profit (some carriers try to whittle even that down).

Yet, many of these contractors also cannot tell you what their actual overhead is or what their net profit was for last year. Like many businesses, the property restoration industry has it's ebbs and flows.

Knowing your slow and peak seasons is helpful so that you understand when to bid projects "heavy" to account for the squeeze on your resources and when to sharpen your pencil so that you can keep your teams working without taking on a loss or dipping below the threshold for your organization.

Whether you are a small business or large, you need to have a firm grasp on what you overhead is. In simple terms, what is the bottom line cost that you have to cover in order to keep the lights on, the vehicles running, your people paid for the hard work that they are doing and a little bit left over so that you can invest in new equipment, raises and other expenses?

The power of a good estimate according to Annissa Coy[41], the Queen of Contents and owner of Firehouse Education:

> *"Correct estimates are critical on every single job not only for the sake of getting paid correctly, but also for maintaining and building relationships with insurance companies and adjusters."*

CHAPTER 14:

Estimating with Xactimate
Commandment 10

Thou Shalt Learn To Master The Trifecta Of Service, Expedience And Accuracy.

Restoration creates the challenge of getting in and getting out expediently while providing a quality service and communicating with multiple shareholders. In program work, there are timeline requirements for specific updates and completion of the project and the team is graded on achieving these objectives. When the scope of work falls outside of the timeline requirements be sure to communicate and update the carrier representatives frequently.

If you are independent, you may not have to deal with the ticking clock and update requirements from the third party administrators, but your client still has their own expectations about project duration. It is important in either scenario to ensure that you communicate realistic expectations, follow up with all parties via emails and ensure you have a paper trail of documentation to support your efforts.

Restoration professionals have to be skilled in the technical aspects of multiple disciplines across their mitigation and repairs service lines. Team members must be able to provide a high level of customer service for their clients. The expectation from carriers is grounded in communication which requires updates across a myriad of industry tools that are often specific to each carrier.

In residential work, it is important to update all parties that own and/or reside at the home being restored. You can get yourself into a lot of needless trouble by assuming that partners are communicating consistently and clearly with each other. Think of your own home, do you always tell your partner everything and in the same level of detail that you received it?

If you have a conversation with one partner, be sure that you follow up with an email to all partners/parties so that everyone has the opportunity to be on the same page. It may sound like extra work but it will help keep you out of a he-said vs. she-said scenario where no one wins.

In commercial work, the decisions may be less personal as often the occupants don't live in the structure (other than apartments), but communication is still essential. Have conversations with all parties and create a mental organization chart so that you understand the roles, responsibilities and authority of each of the players involved in the claim.

In both residential and commercial work, establish the preferred means of communication, whether you will have regular physical meetings and who needs to be apprised of what level of detail. As soon as you are able, set as detailed a production plan as you believe the project requires. I would recommend spending time with this aspect as it will help you think through the process, help set your team up for success and help clarity the expectations of your clients.

Service (external)

Service is a premium in the property restoration business. Often we place a precedence on technical skill when this is perhaps the simplest of the skills to train whereas a person who understands how to connect with customers and serve their needs holds a unique set of skills that is difficult to teach. The customer experience starts with employee engagement.

I had the honor of speaking on this topic with Eric "The Tech Whisperer" Sprague and Larry "Pineapple Man" Wilberton on their podcast Blue Collar Nation[42]. As owners of Shamrock Restoration, Eric and Larry learned that you need to market to your employees as aggressively and consistently as you market to your clients. If you don't believe me, listen to them share it from their experience of successfully bundling and selling their business.

How the customer perceives their experience with your company is as important, if not more important, than the service you provide. I use the example all the time that we could have average to above average carpenters who would do quality work, perhaps not top notch, but the customer loved them and looked over small imperfections because of the relationship and service that carpenter provided.

Conversely, we may have a subcontractor who is phenomenally talented but because they didn't spend the few extra minutes to make the customer feel valued they will pick apart their nearly flawless work.

It's important to understand the value of service in this industry. It's essential in every industry. Your ability to recruit and train people who will help you develop a customer experience that sets you apart from your counterparts only grows in importance as the market gets increasingly competitive. Invest in your people and your process so that you can make progress.

Many companies are hesitant to maintain in-house carpenters because of the cost and their inability to control the labor hours. In my experience, you can control the schedule when your labor is in-house and you have more influence over the experience if you have a strong training system. With subs, you have more control over the cost, but your grip on schedule and customer experience is much lower.

I am sure there are people who would argue against it, but I believe a strong in-house team will lead to longer term success. Even if you use subcontractors, your customers hired your company and will want representation to guide the experience. Many of the companies that I see thriving in the value proposition have found a way to blend these two components.

Service (Internal)

Don't overlook the younger and/or current generations as they are often trainable and adaptable to what you are working to achieve. With the right structure, you can clarify the roles and responsibilities that suit making progress toward your vision and goals so that you distinguish character traits as well as skills that will help you towards those ends.

You may think I am too optimistic about recruiting, hiring and building a team. I am not. I assure you I am not. When I moved to Seattle, at least 70% of my time was spent in recruiting, hiring, firing and doing it again. It was exhausting but it had to be done. I had the chance to sit down with my replacement and he was lamenting the need for good people. I shared with him that you can view it as a burden or a mission, but recruitment is critical to building your vision.

If you need people you can't sit on your butt and expect them to show up. I was able to build up our team by hunting. I scoured LinkedIn, Facebook and Craigslist. I begged our team for referrals. I chased people down at the gas station and the grocery store. I handed more cards out to potential hires than potential clients.

If you are a manager, your job never ends and I believe your ability to make progress is affected by the people you hire and develop to help you continue building. I heard some time ago, "Hire to vision, not to need." I take this to mean that one of the worst things you can do is to hire someone just to fill a roster spot.

I've done this many times and it rarely works out. Hiring just to get a warm body is an energy and resource drain. You and your team will do much better to be lean and mean for a few more weeks than to make a bad hire. It may not seem like it at times, but it's true.

We hired, we fired.

We built, we tore down.

We won, we lost.

We laughed, we cried.

We tried and we tried.

And then we did it again.

Expedience

Expedience is perhaps the most measured of the expectations for restoration contractors, it seems the process is never fast enough for clients or carriers. Even though the age old saying is, "You can have it good, fast or cheap. Pick two." The modern customer, whom I believe is influenced by the unrealistic expectations of the home remodeling shows on TV, expects all three.

You will have to do some patient re-education of your clients expectations to discuss lead times for those deluxe cabinets that they want for their dream kitchen and the subsequent process for measuring, forming and installing their unique stone counters.

One that always makes me pause is the home renovation where the ceramic or stone tile floor is prepped, laid, grouted and sealed in the same day. You will want to discuss the proper steps and timelines for the materials you are installing.

I remember reading that Amazon CEO Jeff Bezos finds it helpful to ask, "What won't change?[43]" He knows that customers will always want lower prices, wider selection and faster delivery. These expectations are a constant. Jeff knows he will never have a customer come to him and say, "Jeff, I love Amazon; I just wish the prices were a little higher. I love Amazon; I just wish you'd deliver a little more slowly."

While client expectations may be unrealistic, we have to hear them and find ways to address them. As professionals, we must develop means of communication that enable us to partner with our customers to achieve outcomes that are mutually beneficial.

On Pro vs. Joe 003 (which is also The DYOJO Podcast Episode

18), Bryan discusses how they realized their job as owners/managers is to ensure that their systems are optimized to keep their employees producing revenue. For them this means improving their ability to create accurate materials lists, stock key items in their warehouse and minimize additional trips to the supply store for missed details.

Efficiency leads to increased productivity (or offsets loss of productivity) which produces a better customer experience and leads to greater profitability (by reducing waste). While many people focus on making the process faster, this may lead to getting the job done more quickly but often can have the unintended consequence of encouraging the team to cut corners to achieve speed at any cost. Be careful with your phrasing and your trading to relay the importance of strategic efficiency rather than heedless expediency.

Key efficiency pickups include:

A consistent client intake process that works to screen unprofitable projects and provide those responding with as many details as can be acquired to set them up for success.

A thorough and clear estimate composed with an accurate diagram, detailed photographs and F9 notes that help the production team decipher nuanced aspects of the project.

When project management operates around ensuring the production team has the details, materials and equipment they need to arrive on the job prepared and stay there until the work is completed. So much time and resources are lost when the production team has to leave the sight for a reason that could have been avoided.

Scope clarity at time of estimating, prior to production and throughout the change order process. As discussed, scope creep includes loss of production due to lack of clarification by the estimator/project manager as well as the lack of capture and communication of job site changes to the work scope.

Accuracy

Most of what we have been discussing up to this point in the 10 Commandments of Xactimate Estimating Success have touched on various aspects of accuracy - such as sketching, photos, line items and communication. As we discussed in Chapter 9, the process of mastery includes *doing it right, doing it efficiently and doing it excellently.* If you are going to do it, do it right and find a way to do it with some class and some sass.

The ability to accurately and effectively communicate the story of the loss and advocate for your approach to a claim are critical to your success as a restoration professional. If you are new to the industry, understand the importance of documentation and that as you move up the ladder the quantity and quality of your documentation is greater, never less.

If you want to build a career in this industry, take pride in your documentation and do your work with excellence. People in a position of leadership need to be able to guide their team members through the process of rolling with the punches to achieve positive outcomes. Managers must build clarity, consistency and accountability in their process if they want progress towards the team objectives.

A contractor's role in the insurance world is to assist the

client with restoring their damaged property to pre-loss conditions, no more and no less. If your client wants upgrades, this is not the responsibility of the carrier so it becomes a separate process. Whether you are a program contractor or independent, it is best to capture these significant changes to the scope of work before the project has started.

When restoration becomes remodeling, the estimator needs to understand there is a different approach and a greater need to clarify the scope, estimate, process and expectation. Insurance companies pay to restore to pre-loss conditions, so the client will be responsible to pay for those items which fall outside of these parameters. Make sure both you as the estimator and the client do not get confused about what the insurance company is and/or isn't paying for.

While the revenue and margins can be better in these upscale projects, these also will require additional attention to materials selection, production schedules and capturing of the details related to changes. Estimators need to be aware of these common scenarios and the organization should develop a strategy for whether they are restorers, remodelers or a mix of both. This obviously isn't the step-by-step guide for the process but in view of mindset and habits for estimating success it is important to be aware and to think through your teams approaches.

Understanding whether it is in your best interest to narrow down to a niche within the market or to provide an extensive menu of services is a discussion that you should have with your team. Monitor where you are most profitable and try to optimize these areas. Without good data, you will struggle to make good decisions. Big numbers in the revenue column do not guarantee the production of quality numbers in achieving profitability.

Nothing More And Nothing Less

Mark Cornelius[44], President at Emergency Mitigation Technician Academy (EMTA):

> "I have been around a bit. Many people believe that if you are not arguing you are leaving money on the table. I have in 35 years done extraordinarily little arguing. No one wins in an argument and it wastes precious time.
>
> Instead of worrying about how much you can charge for the hammer, learn how to use the hammer to its utmost capabilities. Become the most proficient person on the planet with that hammer. The money takes care of itself.
>
> Do what needs to be done, nothing more and nothing less.
>
> Charge for what you did, nothing more and nothing less."

CHAPTER 15

Insurance claims estimating mastery starts with knowing the guidelines of Xactimate.

W hen Moses came down from Mount Sinai with the two stone tablets, there were questions and fear, but there were also some clear directives. Xactimate and program guidelines generate similar emotions but one cannot argue that there are keys to success when working with the estimating software.

You can argue all you want about who gave the directives, who is interpreting the guidelines and whether the system is fair, but you also had better apply your energy to learning Xatimate's keys to success.

If you are just starting out in your estimating journey, you may find our Three R's of Mastering Xactimate for Beginners to be helpful. Insurance claims are subject to some level of interpretation so mastering the tools of the trade is essential to achieving success with the process.

If you are looking to improve your Xactimate prowess or are tasked with helping others to increase theirs, you will find

Habits of Xactimate Estimating Proficiency to be a helpful guideline for the overall process.

If you are down in the depths of getting your estimates constantly ripped apart by reviewers or rejected by adjusters, you will find some help in *Help! Claims Review Shredded My Estimate*. We discuss the parameters for building an internal response system.

The *10 Commandments of Xactimate Estimating Success* will help you to set up good habits as well as refresh your understanding of the keys that lead to mastery with this industry tool.

If you believe these "commandments" are too cumbersome rather than liberating, think of them conversely before you maintain the status quo and thereby reject the "keys to the kingdom" that we have tried to offer you. *Warning, if you don't normally pick up on sarcasm, most of the following items are dripping with this coating.*

The 10 Commandments Of The Status Quo

Preface:

The best thing you can do to help yourself and your team develop would be to continue to do what you are doing, the status quo is *the state in which* things work best. If you are ever critiqued you should recoil abjectly to any inference that you could improve your perspectives or your approach. Best practice for growth minded leaders is to gather an echo chamber of people who complain about the same things that you do - this will help you to ward off any potential feelings that there may be a better way to do things.

One

Thou shalt sketch inaccurately while using a program whose greatest feature is its ability to quantify and clarify scope based upon the diagram component. It's not your fault if dimensions were missed, that's clearly the fault of the program or the carrier or whomever the current president is if you don't agree with their party.

Two

Thou shalt be stingy with thy digital photography as clearly MB of data are more valuable than the time lost in arguing over poor documentation and/or having to return to a job site to retake supporting photos. Create obstacles for your team to complete their most important tasks by limiting resources and providing little training.

Three

Thou shalt leave thy photos in their default reference settings. You've already put the work into taking the pictures, why would you take a few minutes to label them so that there is no confusion over their purpose in supporting your line items? If the adjuster can't figure out that "IMG.4031" is clearly showing the 1/4" scratch on the custom alder door trim that can only be found in the enchanted forests of such and such plan and thereby require x number of dollars more than a standard line item...well, that's their problem. It definitely isn't yours.

Four

Thou shalt omit F9 notes from your estimate. "Less is more," and this rule of twisted thumbs was intended to guide communication in the insurance claims industry where less information always leads to better outcomes for clients, carriers and contractors. Explaining your line items is like labeling your photos, too much needless additional effort.

Five

Thou shalt ignore the admonition to communicate early and often with carriers. If you perform emergency services, you should continue to wait until the very end to communicate with the carrier and then blame them for responding negatively. Learn to play the victim and always blame everyone else involved with the claim. Blame your technicians, subcontractors, clients and the carriers, but never yourself.

Six

Thou shalt provide thy adjuster with as little information as possible, as late as possible and as infrequently as possible. The common denominator in successful personal and professional relationships is poor communication. Take some acting classes so that you can really sell your abhorrence when people question your billing which provides insufficient details and does not hold up to scrutiny.

Seven

Thou shalt dismiss any guidelines presented by anyone. You

are the professional. You've been telling everyone as much for as many years now. If this carrier representative doesn't know who you think you are then, they are going to find out. Puff your chest out and complain to your team again, they love hearing your negativity - it inspires them to be better people.

Eight

Thou shalt fight the system as thou you were advocating for your livelihood. You are bigger than the multi billion dollar systems that the insurance companies have set up. Your's is the voice that everyone has been waiting to hear to clarify the way the rules should be. You haven't invested in or contributed to organized efforts to change the system but by goodness you had better been listened to or your echo chamber is going to hear about it.

Nine

Thou shalt speak against the tool rather than learn its ways. When you were a carpenter, you took the same approach with your worm drive saw - it bent to your will rather than you learning to operate it safely and respecting its intended purpose. That worked so well and that is why you are crushing it as an estimator and your team loves working from your scopes. You know the way that things should be, if you were in charge of everything.

Ten

Thou shalt learn to voice your frustration to your clients, co-workers and anyone who you think wants to listen. You are a master of the blame game, any issues with your estimate making money are the fault of the adjuster, your project manager, employees or subcontractors. People are always attracted to those that never take responsibility and always blame those who are "beneath" them.

Detached Leaders Enable Cultures That Harbor Poor Performers.

Incredibly, it often takes more energy to not be clear, consistent and accountable. The results are frustrating and exhausting. If you have been unintentional and detached for some time you may have an uphill battle, but if you will engage with your passion, pursue your vision and allow your team to assist you in building a culture of excellence you will begin to enjoy the process more.

As Skylar Lewis shares in The DYOJO Podcast Episode 19, you may find that some of the people whom you thought were superstars are not that great of a fit for the new direction. Be careful that you aren't carelessly throwing babies out with the bath water.

When those in a position of leadership are detached from their people, process, production and progress, a lot of leaches like to hide in the dark places within the organization. Clarity and consistency begin to shine a light and reveal attitudes, disciplines and characters that are unwilling to adapt.

Before you get too wild, check yourself, part of the reason you are in this position is that you contributed to the culture of lowered expectations that enabled this environment. You have to own it. You have to deconstruct and rebuild. Thankfully we are really good at doing this with structures, but we make it more difficult than it needs to be with people and organizations.

Two Questions[45] that will help you be a better leader:

As a leader, if you want to ask an effective question, ask yourself, "Am I on course or off track?" This is important because, in order to answer this basic question, you have to establish some clarity as to what your goals are.

If you are clear on your goals, you can develop action steps and track whether you are consistently moving towards or away from your goal. Questions of substance will require you to look in the mirror and assess measurable results.

Am I a leader? **Yes.**

Am I on or off course? **TBD**

The importance of being intentional as a leader.

If you are brave enough to ask yourself whether you are on or off course, you are on your way towards progress in the process. There is one more tough question a person in a position of leadership must ask, especially if your roles and responsibilities have you overseeing a team of people.

"Am I on track due to intention or coincidence?"

The prototypical leader enjoys receiving praise for success and shirks responsibility for failures. Whether things are going well or they are a dumpster fire, the person in a position of leadership must ask if their outcomes have been the result of being intentional or merely coincidental.

Is the team winning because you have been intentional in helping them prepare for and achieve success?

Are things going well in spite of your efforts (or lack thereof) as a person in a position of leadership?

Leadership is a daily process.

You are a leader. You have a responsibility to lead yourself, master your roles, execute your responsibilities and set a positive example for others. If you want to grow as a person and be effective in your leadership, ask yourself whether you are on course or off course.

If you are on track to reach your objectives, have you done everything in your power to be intentional with your efforts and empowering those around you to succeed? If you are off track, move towards being intentional by facing the music and set an example of climbing out of your mess. It's never too late to take a step in the right direction.

Stop asking dumb questions and start doing intentional things. As the process evolves, you will have to adapt, so the development of your leadership skills is never over. If you work through the process of taking ownership of your role as a leader, getting yourself and your team on course and being intentional, it's not as though the game is over.

Repeat daily.

The Best And The Worst

Andrew McCabe, The Godfather of Remote Estimating[46], owner of Claims Delegates and seasoned Xactimate professional:

> *"The best estimators have spent a lot of time around other estimators. They have been exposed to many approaches and have the ability to adopt those things that benefit them the most. The worst estimators aren't estimators at all; they're data input. Their sheets all look the same. They've decided that they have the same things they use on every job and don't customize the estimate to the job at hand. Over reliance on macros are a telltale sign of a lazy estimator."*

CHAPTER 16

What can we do to make it better?

Many restoration professionals are frustrated with the current status of the insurance industry. Rather than commiserating with your peers and complaining from the sidelines, what can we do to help bring things into a more sustainable situation?

Feedback to Xactimate

If you want to help get the pricing in Xactimate updated in your market, Alena Wilson[47] co-founder of XM8 Mastery shares a few key starting points. She says that there are options for contractors to be proactive about the pricing (Xactimate) that is used in this industry.

> *"You can be the change that the industry needs by inform-ing Xactware of the pricing disparities and variations. The contractor can be in the driver's seat, if we all start to give the feedback through Xactware's channels."*

Complete your estimates

You can help influence this pricing by starting to mark your estimates as "Complete" in Xactimate. Every time you make a price change to a line item then mark the estimate as "Complete," you are submitting data that is included in the top-down pricing methodology.

Make pricing discrepancies known

You may also contact the pricing department with a price discrepancy that you see on a daily basis. For example, you see that the line item for painting deck railing does not seem to include enough labor to paint railing, balustrade, bottom rail, etc.

You may email pricing@xactware.com to give them your labor rate for this type of work and help with the bottom-up pricing methodology. The pricing department will typically get back with you within 24 hours with a decision on how they are going to use your data to help with that line item's labor pricing.

Option 5

You may also call the Pricing department at 800-424-9228 Option 5 to discuss pricing data and discrepancies with Xactware directly. They are open for feedback and welcome contractors to call and give them notice that pricing is low for a certain area.

Collaboration for industry advocacy

Writing in the Restoration Advocacy Report #3[48], Ed Cross comments that the advocacy efforts of the Restoration Industry Association (RIA) Advocacy and Government Affairs Committee (AGA), and the industry as a whole, must be pursued, "Aggressively, but diplomatically and ethically," in order to create sustainable solutions for all stakeholders.

By synthesizing the feedback from restoration professionals, the AGA identified four key focus areas and subsequently created four subcommittees:

Pricing

TPA (third party administrators)

Investments

TPC (third party consultant)

You can contribute financially[49] to the RIA's efforts as well as volunteer to be a member of one of these committees where your experience and passion may be best utilized for the good of all. Progress is evident as RIA President Mark Springer has recently conducted three Industry Briefing calls regarding Xactimate Pricing.

Mark and AGA Chairwoman Katie Smith have curated this discussion, exclusively for RIA members, with Xactware President, Mike Fulton. The RIA notes on their website that,

> *"Mike has acknowledged that contractors have different overhead needs and the right price is job specific. Xactware is listening to our feedback and working with us to improve their tools to reflect more accurate rates[50]."*

<u>Property Restoration Peer Networking Groups include (alphabetical order):</u>

Alliance of Independent Restorers (AIR[51])

"The Alliance of Independent Restorers isn't just a group –

it's a movement. Our mission is to take back the restoration industry. We are an association of like-minded, honest, and empowered professionals who are aligned in encouraging the success of each member."

International Cleaning and Restoration Association (ICRA[52])

"ICRA streamlines and promotes the efforts of cleaning and restoration associations, their collective membership, and other industry partners, by providing leadership, collaboration, educational programs and support/ benefit services that are vital to their business interests, growth, success, and profits."

National Organization of Restoration and Remediation Professionals (NORRP[53])

"Our goal is to keep every individual in the industry as up to date on the most advanced techniques, most current equipment, and the best methods for billing and estimating projects in order to ensure the proper progression of our industry."

The Restoration Association (TRA[54])

"The Restoration Association exists to build a community of restoration professionals and affiliates with local chapters that add value and harvest new ideas, not to make a profit off of memberships."

Restoration Industry Association (RIA[55])

"The oldest and largest non-profit, professional trade as-

sociation dedicated to providing leadership and promoting best practices through advocacy, standards & professional qualifications for the restoration industry."

Restoration Rebels[56]

"To elevate our industry through enhanced education and technologies and create a community of vetted restoration specialists who leverage the network to grow their business. United we're strong. Divided we're weak."

Education is key to success

Benjamin Franklin is credited with saying, "An investment in knowledge pays the best interest." Mr. Franklin wanted to be a writer but couldn't afford a tutor so he devised a method for improving his skills, he basically would copy esteemed writers from The Spectator to marinate in their flow and vocabulary.

"I took some of the papers, and, making short hints of the sentiment in each sentence, laid them by a few days, and then, without looking at the book, try'd to compleat [sic] the papers again, by expressing each hinted sentiment at length, and as fully as it had been expressed before, in any suitable words that should come to hand[57]."

While copying and presenting the text as your own is plagiarism, many artists learn by first emulating their heroes. I know I learned to draw first by tracing and adapting new styles by trying to copy from artists that I revered. Many popular bands started out doing cover songs as a means to learn structure, rhythm and style. Apparently The Rolling Stones[58] and Panic! At the Disco started out this way before becoming successful worldwide brands.

Educate yourself and your team in the ways of Xactimate. There are classes you can take from reputable trainers who know the industry and the tool. Simple internal tools, as have been suggested throughout this book, will help you elevate your game whether that is having another estimator review your proposal or developing a more formal process for your team.

It's better to have some consistent internal review before you face the shark infested waters of external rejections. Just remember, don't hate the players, who are just doing their job, if you are truly frustrated - work to improve the system.

Educational resources for Xactimate include:

This book. Share it on your social media and tell your friends about all the things that you have learned!

Actionable Insights provides a monthly Xactimate price list update summary[59] to help keep you informed on what has changed within this resource.

Enlightened Restoration Solutions offers Xactimate training courses[60] and a Pricing feedback webinar from Ben Justesen.

Xactware provides a variety of training options[61] to pursue Xactimate certification.

The DYOJO has a resource page for Property Restoration[62] which includes articles and videos on Xactimate success.

Property Restoration And Service Based Podcasts:

Podcasts can supplement your personal and professional development, here are a few from our friends:

IAQ Radio[63] is the OG of the property restoration web based audio content. Joe "Radio Joe" Hughes and Cliff "The Z Man" Zlotnik host the show, which is recorded live every Friday at noon Eastern Standard Time.

Gerrett Stier is a great person with a killer product, The GMS Podcast[64] creates the atmosphere of friends discussing their life experiences and the details of their unique services.

The DYOJO Podcast, which is the DO Your Job Dojo, brings entertaining and inspiring guests who will help you laugh and learn as you shorten your learning curve in the property restoration industry.

Eric "The Tech Whisperer" Sprague and Larry "Pineapple Man" Wilberton share the keys that helped them start, grow and successfully sell their restoration company on their Blue Collar Nation Podcast. They have recently started Blue Collar Nation Radio[65] which is a 24/7 collection of content for service based businesses.

The Claim Clinic[66] podcast is a master class for property restoration professionals from Andrew McCabe, author of The 24 Hour Tech.

Straight Talk[67] is a webcast from Jeff Cross, the editorial director of ISAA Media which also produces Cleanfax as well as Cleaning and Maintenance Magazine.

Pro vs. Joe is a podcast within a podcast from The DYOJO Podcast. For those new to the industry, you will receive a crash course in building your business. For those who have been in the industry for sometime, you will find that the conversation re-ignites your passion for the good work that our teams do day-in and day-out.

CHAPTER 17

Habits of Xactimate Estimating Proficiency

How often have you heard that the purpose of the estimate is to tell the story of the loss? If you haven't heard that yet, please lock it into your brain's memory bank now. When writing an estimate in Xactimate, your opening statement is the start of that story narrative. This introduction to the overview of the claim should give anyone browsing your estimate a synopsis of the source of the loss, extent of the damages and your approach to restoring the property.

A concise opening narrative also provides an outline of the structure for a solid Xactimate estimate. If you follow our process, you will start from the source of the loss outward. As you compose your line items, you will either write your estimate in a sequence from the top down or the bottom up. You will create headers that give your estimates an aesthetic that leads the reviewer through a guided tour of the damages in each room. Your F9 notes and photos will supplement any line items that create questions for the carrier.

When you write in a consistent manner, you help yourself to reduce the chance of missed scope details. When you compose in a clear structure you are attempting to minimize the questions that a reviewer might ask. It can be frustrating when you put so much effort into an estimate and silly questions still get asked, but if you continue to work with those entities they will come to appreciate the level of detail that you provide.

It is possible to stand out when composing estimates in Xactimate. It may not happen often, but it is alway nice to hear someone say, "I really like how your estimate is structured. That's the first estimate in a long time that had a flow to it that I could follow. You really are the best and there is no one like you. I hope your boss is paying you well because you are worth every cent and more. I want to be like you when I grow up."

Maybe I embellished a little there, but you get the idea. We don't live for the approval of others, but it is nice to be recognized.

Poorly structured estimates show a lack of care and/or expertise

How often have you reviewed an estimate from an adjuster or a competitor that has little structure and is hard to follow? There are so many estimates that look like a grenade full of line items was thrown into the program and exploded. It's like mystery night when someone extracts all the leftovers from the refrigerator and attempts to make something edible.

How many of you are reading this and know that those same poorly structured estimates are being composed by your hands or those of your team members? Most Xactimate professionals can see the telltale signs of an estimator who is either inexperienced or is lazy in their estimating habits:

Rooms that are sketched as separate entities that are not connected as a monolithic structure. This isn't sketching, it's sketchy (how's that for an estimator joke?). Poor diagraming habits demonstrate that you do not have mastery of the platform.

Minimal photographs and no labeling to assist with associating the picture with the scope. A lack of photos is a sure fire way to get your estimate rejected, whether you are doing program work or are an independent.

Estimates with line items that are non-sequential, this is a chaotic way to approach an estimate and does not help a reviewer to follow the story of the loss. I believe it is a greater waste of time to compose estimates in this way as the chaos will filter through to your production team.

If you are lost or this is the first time you are hearing of such things, please refer to the chapter titled The Three R's of Mastering Xactimate for more guidance.

Structural habits will help generate estimating consistency

Many Xactimate professionals are fans of macros. While I have several friends who utilize these tools, I have often found that they are more cumbersome than they are helpful. You will have to decide for yourself what works best for you and your team. With credit to my former employer BELFOR, who is one of the largest players in the property restoration landscape, they worked to promote estimating consistency which helped to elevate my own habits.

As we have discussed in prior chapters, when you structure your estimate with headers, this helps you as the estimator to capture the details the same way every time. These habits are critical to reducing those missed items that enable you to set up a project for success.

Headings also serve as a sort of table of contents for each room so that reviewers and customers will see both the care you have put into your estimate as well as enable them to follow your approach more clearly. Headers help you compose a more complete estimate, help reviewers to follow the story of the loss and can help your production team execute the plan.

How top-down or bottom-up informs our estimate structure:

If you are working top down, you might start the headings in your estimate as ceilings, walls, fixtures, finishes, flooring and prep items. You can get as detailed as you want by having those core categories capitalized and in bold with sub categories only in bold. For example, a basic header structure in a room might include:

Room: Kitchen

PREP ITEMS:

Masking

Contents

Detach and reset items

WALLS & CEILINGS:

Wall and/or ceiling repairs

If there is significant cabinet work you might make a sub-header

TRIM & PAINT:

Baseboard, casing and/or molding

Prime and paint

FLOORS & CLEANING:

Flooring repairs

Cleaning specific items and openings

Final cleaning

Mitigation headings would include prep items, equipment, removal and monitoring.

Even if you use time and materials for your estimating, you can segment your billing recap by room or area into category headings for a much cleaner and easier to follow estimate. Oftentimes, for larger mitigation projects, I would break out our scope of work with a header for each day or week.

The goal is to tell the story, ensure you don't miss items, help your clients to be able to follow your approach to the loss and set your estimates apart from the status quo. When you are working for a client they want to see the value they are receiving for the cost they are paying. If you complete a large loss and submit a one line invoice, this may not be the best communication of the work that your team did and the value your organization brought to that client.

Setting your estimate apart from the status quo

While there are plenty of tricks of the trade and technological advances that can take your estimating to the next level, it all starts with mastering the basics. Brian Hoyer, who was a back-up for the six time Super Bowl champion quarterback Tom Brady, noted how dedicated Tom was to practicing the basics[68].

> *"Being around it makes you a better quarterback," Hoyer said. "You watch what he does and how focused he is with fundamentals -- front foot, shoulders, eyes, all those things. I remember going back to my first stint here (2009-2011) and I felt like I became such a better fundamental passer just by watching him and doing the same drills. He's obsessed with it."*

Your process as an estimator starts with getting the claim details before you visit the loss site. Following the same process each time as you document the loss through photographs from the front of the loss and on through the structure. Again, you are telling the story and a picture is worth a thousand words so you can never take too many photos.

Your habits should include sketching your estimate the same way each time as well as taking detailed notes while onsite. Once you have the data, it's time to compose your estimate structure and capture the line items that reflect a solid Xactimate estimate. Mastering the fundamentals will set you apart.

This approach to the details should carry through the execution of your project. Whether you are a write-and-run estimator, someone who both writes the estimate as well as sees it through the production phase, then you will want your documentation to tell the story from start to finish.

If your only responsibility is to write the estimate you still want to set your project management team up with good details to help them jump into the project and carry that communication through to the end. Many people call this a communication log. It can be formal or a running notepad of your conversations with the client. If you utilize job numbers, I like to always include the job number in my emails so they are easy to organize and pull up for reference.

Your habits demonstrate your professionalism

As Brian Hoyer notes, Brady's dedication to the fundamentals inspired him to be better. I am so thankful to be a part of an industry where professionals are challenging each other to be better every day. I am also thankful for some great mentors who have demonstrated how to do things the right way and to be proud of doing so. There are national, regional and local groups available in most markets that provide you access to other professionals who have likely been there and done that (BTDT).

Reaching out for help is a sign of strength and the collaboration amongst peers is very positive. I believe this is what makes the Pro vs. Joe Podcast[69] so fun and relevant as Bryan Close "the Joe" and myself, the mediocre "Pro", discuss the nuances of the property restoration industry from our diverse experiences. Our goal is to help others to shorten their DANG learning curve for professional development.

Good competition is good for all of us and elevates our industry. As Mark Whatley says on The DYOJO Podcast Episode 9[70], "Rising tides raise all ships." Whether you are starting your estimating journey, improving your Xactimate skills or managing other estimators, my hope is that this book is one of many resources that help you on your journey. Continue your professional development by mastering the basics, learning from your peers and setting an example of excellence for those around you.

Forming Estimating Habits

Kirk Matthews, owner of Oregon Valley and Coastal Claim Service[71], shares a few simple fixes that are indicative of bad habits by estimators:

Too many "LAB" hours – sometimes supplemental labor hours are justified, but too often it's just laziness.

"Close enough" line items. It's bad form if an estimator uses a line item when it doesn't match the scope of work being outlined.

Wording in explanations, such as opening statements and F9 notes, are often needlessly aggressive. It is much better to teach rather than sell.

Inserting your own pricing without an explanation or justification for the alteration.

Using masking line items when you've already demoed the entire room. Use line items in a sequence that makes sense with the scope you are creating.

Over use of energized terms such as 'microbial growth', when other items may be better suited to covered claims such as Category 3 line items.

Too much ego. Everyone makes mistakes. No need to drag someone through the mud due to an error. These estimates are intricate, and errors happen.

CHAPTER 18

Help! Claims Review Shredded
My Estimate.

"They've shredded my estimate!" Exclaimed Estimator #1.

"Again?" Replies his peer, Fellow Estimator.

"It's like they take joy in their sadistic responses." Estimator #1 progresses from shock to anger.

"So brutal." Fellow Estimator commiserates.

They literally took my restoration estimate and ran it through a cheese grater." Estimator #1 continues to wallow in misery.

"How do they expect us to make any money?" Fellow Estimator attempts to console their compatriot.

Fellow Estimator knows that their estimate will soon be the next victim of the insurance review gauntlet. They know that the next time they send an estimate to a reviewer or hit upload in Xactimate, the process will run its cycle with them.

Have you been in this room before?

If you work around insurance claims, you know this scenario is a common one in many restoration companies. Perhaps your own bruises are still turning purple and your wounds are still bleeding. We all have choices to make. We can play the status quo game and join our peers, Estimator #1 and Fellow Estimator, in their glum state or we can work to find answers.

Many of you are saying, "We have tried." If you will journey with me a bit further into this scenario, perhaps we can assess our effort and dive a bit deeper into making progress in the process.

What would the typical response be as this scenario plays itself out?

"Who are they to question me?" Estimator #1 rises indignantly and then rattles off a hastily worded email.

"This claims review 'professional' has never been to this job – they've probably never been to any job site ever." Fellow Estimator exclaims.

Funny enough, this is both one of the issues as well as one of the keys to resolution as well. The person reviewing Estimator #1's estimate has never been to this job. Claims Reviewer #1 works from a claims center half-way across the country.

Claims Reviewer #1 likely hasn't been to any job and possibly never will. It's not their job. This is a fact of the process and it does no good to complain about it.

Their titles do not put them at odds, one writes an estimate for the claim and the other reviews the estimate for the claim. They may view their responsibility to be at odds with each other but that is not inherent to the task at hand. The presiding principle should be to restore the client to pre-loss conditions and both parties should be working together to make this as expedient as possible.

The difference between what should be and what is leaves a lot of room for us to work towards a process that is clear and consistent. We can start by asking better questions.

"What are the objections of Claims Reviewer #1?" Estimator Supervisor asks.

"Who invited you?" questions Fellow Estimator.

"My company header isn't in the estimate," replies Estimator #1.

Have you experienced this rejection note? It seems silly but it's a requirement. Should anyone on the contractor side be upset with the claims review process if they have not updated their program to have the correct company information in their estimate headers? Whose responsibility is it to ensure that their organization is following the basic requirements for carriers and programs?

Company	Wins	Losses	Ties
Restoration Company #1	0	1	0

Issue: Poor carrier and program basic level compliance.
Response: Clear training and consistent processes for estimate compliance.

"It appears that Claims Reviewer #1 composed a detailed list of their reasons for the rejection of your estimate. What is the next objection?" inquires Estimator Supervisor.

"My opening statement does not provide sufficient details per the carrier requirements," Estimator #1 reads with a quizzical tone in their voice.

While we are laboring into the weeds a bit here we are also discussing elements of Insurance Claims 101. These are common rejection items that are easily addressed and yet continue to be hang ups for restoration companies large and small. If you read our article on the *Habits of Xactimate Estimating Success*, we outlined how your estimate is part of telling the story of the claim.

As estimators we have the responsibility to learn how to tell the story of the loss through the estimating tool that we use. The estimate has a language. Do you remember when you first sat down with Xactimate? It can seem like a foreign language. What is WTR EQD? What does HMR BARR mean? When is the right time to use PNT MSKLF?

Whether you like it or not, for the majority of insurance claims, Xactimate has become the recognized story delivery tool. When our story does not resonate with our audience we need to learn how to communicate more clearly. In serving our client, it is necessary to use the resources in our tool bag to assist them in achieving a well executed outcome.

If your estimate is not compliant with basic carrier requirements, rejection is not the result of sadism, it's the consequence of self-sabotage.

Company	Wins	Losses	Ties
Restoration Company #1	0	2	0

Issue: Poor execution of initial estimate components.
Response: Better attention to details. Learn to become a better claims story teller.

"They are picking apart my line items," Estimator #1 yells, pounding a fist against their desk.

"They do that to me all the time," Fellow Estimator raises their hands in disgust.

"I remember when I used to be an estimator…" Estimator Supervisor starts to chime in, thinking that they are a part of the group grievance session only to be interrupted.

"No one cares about what you did eighty years ago!" both Estimator #1 and Fellow Estimator blurted out.

We are now entering much more subjective territory. There are ongoing discussions about the best ways to approach insurance claims work from various levels of the business. Resources like Restoration & Remediation Magazine (R&R) do a great job of giving a voice to industry leaders and their experiences.

Let's discuss a few options when faced with opposition from an insurance reviewer:

Estimate Rejection Response Option #1

Dig our heels in. There are those of the mind that the carrier can never be right and the claims process is a war. If they want to question us we will know the fine print better than them and will throw it at them with everything that we have.

If your organization has agreed to do program work then some of these line item concessions are part of the contractual agreement. This is why some companies have chosen to stay independent and refuse to engage in third party administrator (TPA) work. If you a person in a position of leadership you will have to decide if the potential volume is worth the tradeoff.

Estimate Rejection Response Option #2

Give in to expedite. Some professionals believe that a quick claim that is paid in part is better than a drawn out battle. Many of the organizations that regularly work with carriers or TPA's exercise some level of pragmatism.

As noted previously, the theory is that concessions will be made to build a relationship that will result in a volume of work that will outweigh the costs. For many of these companies this is survival mode, "We don't know what we would do without program work so we have to do what it takes to keep the funnel open."

Estimate Rejection Response Option #3

Get educated. Whether you work with a TPA or are doing direct work for carriers, after a few claims you typically get a sense for the line items that are more likely to get rejected or questioned. Know your program outlines, your carrier specifics and what sequences can be approved (or overridden) by adjuster authorization.

If you have a claim that requires a unique approach you should be in contact early and regularly with the adjuster to confirm authorization for your approach to assisting their client with a positive outcome.

Develop your process intentionally.

Do some research.

Tap into your peer network.

Communicate with the adjuster early and often.

Make progress in your process.

Were Keith Richards and Mick Jagger in the property restoration business prior to forming The Rolling Stones? Did they have insurance estimate reviews in mind when they penned the timeless words, "You can't get what you want. But if you try sometimes, well, you might find you get what you need."

If you write a sloppy estimate and you are not learning from prior mistakes, expect to get rejected. At the same time, whenever the carrier or program initiates a rejection of an estimate this should be a time where the restorer reviews whether the objections are legitimate. This invitation to review the merit of the estimate is also a time when the estimator should review whether legitimate line items were missed in the prior submission.

Company	Wins	Losses	Ties
Restoration Company #1	0	2	1

Issue: Lack of clarity regarding proper use of line items relevant to the claim.
Response: Skills development through research, peers and training as well as learning from prior rejections.

"They are saying we don't have sufficient supporting photos,"

Estimator Supervisor states looking up from the computer screen.

"Oh, and the photos that were uploaded aren't properly labeled or associated with the rooms in which they were taken," continues Fellow Estimator.

"What?" queries Estimator #1.

If a photo is worth a thousand words, in the world of insurance claims those photos could be thousands of dollars. One hundred dollars (or even less) can be the tipping point between a profitable project and a net loss. A clearly written estimate that follows industry guidelines must have supporting photo documentation – we aren't yet talking about high level Xactimate skills.

Estimators must be storytellers. Our audience likes their stories to be full of vibrant pictures that are captioned. Often we are communicating our claim stories to persons who will not be physically present at the loss. Pictures help the claim story to come to life for them. Develop your ability to tell a story and to support your story with multiple photos that are clearly labeled to illustrate your narrative. The more detailed or unique the work you need to complete the more quantitative as well as qualitative your photographs need to be.

Company	Wins	Losses	Ties
Restoration Company #1	0	3	1

Issue: Poor illustrative support for proposed scope of work.
Response: As you develop your story telling abilities, make sure your stories are packed with good pictures.

If we have a losing mindset and we maintain the status quo of losing habits, we will continue to lose. Estimators have a job to do. Claims review professionals have a job to do. Organizations have a responsibility to train their people to execute with excellence when it comes to carrying out the essential functions of their roles.

"I don't know what I am going to do," Estimator #1 is on the verge of tears, "No matter how I respond they are going to tear me to pieces."

"When the claims reviewer shreds your estimate, it's time to make tacos!"

"Who said that?" Fellow Estimator yells into the abyss.

Suddenly, they can hear a familiar tune, "You can't always get what you want..."

"But if you try sometimes," Estimator #1 bobs their head.

"Is it lunch time?" Estimator Supervisor asks as they leave the room.

Unfortunately, more often than not, our responses to the estimate review process borders on burying our head in the sand or playing the victim. We throw our hands up and rail against the system. As noted above, we can choose to go to war, we can choose to give in or we can choose to get educated. Neither of these decisions guarantee success.

Going to war will have casualties, giving in will cost you and getting educated does not mean that everyone will admire your knowledge to the point that they will see things your way. You may feel like you have lost in the past but today is a new day, it's time for a new approach – the "scoreboard" is blank (but the clock is ticking).

Company	Wins	Losses	Ties
Restoration Company #1	0	0	0

Issue: Frustration with the claims review process.
Resolution: Gather data that will inform decisions so that progress can be made.

Simple Data Will Help You Drive Change

So, how do we gain ground on the claims review process? Here are some suggestions to start tracking data to inform decisions and find resolution:

Do you review your rejections for trends? You can do this as a team or you can do this as an individual estimator. You can download the attached PDF Tracking Claims Review Worksheet (see end of article) or you can develop your own system.

Change your mindset. Above we framed the claims review process in wins, losses and ties. With this win-loss mindset our sample restoration company was not winning. What if we change our mindset to founded (reasonable review queries based upon the standards, practices and carrier guidelines), unfounded (contradictory to standards, practices and carrier guidelines) or in the gray area (subject to interpretation). If you download our worksheet you will notice these are the categories.

Change your process. The status quo is to complain about the system. If you are approaching your profession with a growth mindset you will work to find solutions to your issues. Start by tracking your rejections so that you can make decisions based upon objective data rather than your collective-subjective opinions.

Items in Review	Founded	Unfounded	Gray Area	Resolution

You do insurance work.

Claims review is part of the process.

Our point here is not that insurance is right or that contractors are wrong, but that if we want to achieve progress in the process we have to control what we can control. Take ownership for roles and responsibilities.

If you are not collecting data on your rejections you should start immediately.

If you have data you need to use it to help educate your decisions so that you can gain ground.

This conversation here is regarding mindset and process. Start gathering data so that you can make more informed decisions and work to find resolutions. Regardless of your chosen approach, develop your process intentionally.

Check out The DYOJO's *Tracking Claims Review Worksheet* available as a Free PDF[72] download from our website.

EPILOGUE

Naming a book is a difficult thing. I wouldn't say there is as much weight to it as naming your children, but there is a similar sense in which you want the name to convey the spirit, the content and the character of the book. As such, I went through several names which I thought might be entertaining for you to read as you ponder whether this book was useful or not.

Name 1

The Keys to the Insurance Restoration Kingdom

I had this vision of the semi-classic video game *Out-Run* with the blond haired male driver racing through various landscapes in his Magnum PI Ferrari. I thought this might even be a cool cover to connect with a 90's kid vibe and our base of contractors. But I wondered if people would get the reference or connect with the vibe? Being too niche can be risky.

The name was too long so I contemplated either The Keys to the Kingdom with a snappy subtitle. I also considered a Sword in the Stone theme as many view Xactimate as more of a burden than a resource. But I didn't want to be confused for a children's book as I am sure googling "Sword in the Stone" would not bring potential readers to my musings in an SEO battle with Disney.

Subtitle

Establishing the Right Mindset and Habits for Yourself and Your Team to Succeed with Estimating Insurance Claims.

There was never really a doubt about the subtitle. Your subtitle needs to be self-explanatory and give the buyer/reader an opportunity to decide whether they are "in" or "out" when it comes to purchasing your contribution to the literary community. I wanted to set the expectation that this is about **mindset** and **habits** rather than a how-to when it comes to estimating

Names 2, 3 & 4

I walked by a cookware store while on an outing with my children and saw a book titled "You Suck at Cooking". I love this type of snark and while I did not buy the book I did take a picture.

Jeff Moore from ATI shared that several of the title options I expressed gave him this same feeling, that they make him laugh but they don't make him want to buy the book. A key insight. Thank you Jeff.

I was tempted to name it **You Suck at Estimating** but that was too much of a direct rip off. So I played around with these two derivations:

How to not suck at estimating - A book of the estimators, for the estimators and by the estimators.

This played on two levels, it was a nod to the irreverence of the cooking book that caught my attention in the display window while adding a patriotic gesture towards the language of the Declaration of Independence.

The dichotomy of being an estimator - that we have to know our history, follow the guidelines and yet rage against the system in tactful ways as we build our careers. So, this became the official sub-sub title of the book.

The guide to not being the worst estimator in the history of estimating as you build your own legacy of estimating success in a world of mediocre estimators.

I also think that ridiculously long names are funny or perhaps the influence of writers the likes of Dr. Suess who share wisdom in unique packages. There is something special about finding someone who has yet to be discovered or who exists outside of the mainstream and drops nuggets of knowledge.

Ben Justesen from Enlightened Restoration Solutions suggested that whatever the title was it should be succinct. It is great to have helpful input from industry peers. Thank you Ben.

Name 5

With the help of Michelle Blevins from Restoration and Remediation Magazine (R&R), much of my content falls into the umbrella of being *The Intentional Restorer*. She invented this term as we considered a name form my monthly column and she briliantly played off of the tagline for The DYOJO which is "Develop Intentionally".

If you are not aware, Michelle is always working behind

the scenes to help provide good content to restoration professionals. She was recently a guest on Gerrett Stier's GMS Podcast[73] and will soon be a guest of The DYOJO Podcast.

This book will likely be the first in a potential series of *Be Intentional* scripts. The theme of this one is estimating, as so much of what we do in property restoration is affected by the quality of the estimates being composed.

Whether you are starting your career, working to reach that next level or are tasked with helping your team members develop their skills, I believe you will find this book to be helpful in your efforts. If you find that it does so, please share those experiences with everyone in your network!

Personal and professional development are all the rage. At The DYOJO we want to encourage people:

Don't make things more complicated than they need to be (Reduce 2 Produce[74]).

Take clear, consistent and accountable steps towards your goals (Blueprint 4 Success[75]).

Develop intentionally by asking yourself regularly whether you are on track and if you have been intentional (2 Questions[76]).

This book will help you to be intentional or you can't be helped. I have learned many things about leadership and the two most important are 1) never get to the root of an issue, always just pick at the symptoms and 2) teamwork means you always have someone else to blame...you caught that these two items were sarcastic, right?

Being intentional is the first step, whether you are starting your career, advancing your career, improving your abilities or helping others to develop their skills. Wherever you are, *develop intentionally*. Remember, the status quo includes doing what you've always done, deflecting any criticism onto others and complaining with your buddies about how you wish things were like, "The good ol' days."

Same Terrible Band, Same Sad Tune?

If you are part of the "We've-always-done-it-that-way," traveling road band, you probably have not made it this far in this book as some of these things are so simple and yet they slap against those resistant to criticism, change, adaptation or process improvement.

In contrast, I wrote an article about Bruce Lee and achieving your goals. I was struck by the way in which his quotes punched right through the BS to provide some clarity on the principles of becoming better at anything. Listen to the intentionality in his thought process and execution in this excerpt published in Cleanfax[77]:

Bruce Lee approached martial arts with the thoughtfulness of a philosopher. He was intentional in his actions and his intensity brought a brilliance to everything that he did. Lee expressed several key ideas that are helpful to personal and professional development. Our ability to reach our goals has a lot to do with how well we prioritize our efforts.

Rabid Practicality

"Knowing is not enough, we must apply. Willing is not enough, we must do." - Bruce Lee

Lee wanted Jeet Kun Do to incorporate, "Practicality, flexibility, speed, and efficiency." Personal development is a paradox. To achieve we must be practical as well as rabidly ambitious.

This is best expressed as being led by vision. You should have Big Hairy Audacious Goals (BHAG) but to achieve you must break those down into 10 year, 3 year, 1 year, quarterly, monthly and daily goals. Build your confidence by breaking your dreams into goals and get to work.

Veracious Hunger

"Absorb what is useful, discard what is useless and add what is specifically your own." - Bruce Lee

Bruce was well-read and had an extensive library dominated by martial arts subjects and philosophical texts. Your professional development must be applicable to your vision, this does not mean that you can only study what others in your industry produce. Lee learned from disciplines as broad as fencing and boxing to develop his art. Learn to discern between what is helpful and what is not. Keep making progress in your process.

Aggressive Reduction

"It is not a daily increase, but a daily decrease. Hack away at the inessentials." - Bruce Lee

How often do you have multiple tabs open or too much clutter in your work space? When we realize it is better to have a few things that are completely done than several things that are only partially done, we start to win the battle of prioritization.

Author Stephen Covey frames it this way, The key is not to prioritize what's on your schedule, but to schedule your priorities." Start your day with a plan and work your plan rather than just winging it. Live your life with intentionality.

Unrelenting Belief

"Life's battles don't always go to the stronger or faster man. But sooner or later the man who wins, is the man who thinks he can." - Bruce Lee

In her book Unqualified Success[78], author Rachel Stewart shares personal and practical tips for bridging the gap from where you are today to where you want to be. What is unique about her book is that she walks the reader through portions of her own professional development where she felt unqualified.

Rachel came to realize that we all start out unqualified which should be motivating rather than deflating. Cleaning out your thought closet and taking ownership of your thoughts are keys to unlocking your potential.

Your dreams should fear you

Whether your goal is to build something new as an entrepreneur or to improve your organization's performance as a manager, start by leading yourself. Time is limited so make sure you are using it effectively.

Open a can of intentionality by prioritizing your efforts and resources towards making progress on your goals. There are no short-cuts or secret sauce. Every dreamer can be an achiever. Open a can of motivation by remembering this encouragement from Bruce Lee, "The successful warrior is the average man, with laser-like focus."

As you have probably gathered by reading this, at The DYOJO, we don't do things "by the book". We literally are writing our own book. I believe it is important to take input and insight from others, but you also have to take risks and make some of your own mistakes in order to solidfy the lessons along your journey of personal and professional development.

I hope I have informed and entertained you. I hope you have found this book to dumb. As you will recall, because you have read and retained every word of this manuscript, the definition of dumb is, "To simplify or reduce the intellectual content of something so as to make it accessible to a larger number of people." Do you remember what your Google and/or Kindle (Amazon) reviews should note? I would be honered if you said that this was, "The dumbest book I ever read (all the way through) on this topic."

The DYOJO: *Develop Intentionally.*

ABOUT THE AUTHOR

Jon Isaacson, The Intentional Restorer[11], is a freelance writer, business coach, speaker and 18 year veteran of the property restoration industry. His organization, The DYOJO[12] is the Do Your Job Dojo, which partners with leaders in property restoration to develop people, process, production and progress (4 P's).

Additional resources from Mr. Isaacson include:

The DYOJO Podcast[13] (Spotify, iTunes, Google and Anchor) *INFOtainment helping you shorten your DANG learning curve for professional development.*

The DYOJO Youtube Page

A FREE E-book The 10 Commandments of Xactimate Estimating[14]

Articles in publications which include Claims Pages, Insurance Nerds, Cleanfax, Project Management Times and many more.

Jon has been a recent guest on Gerrett Stier's GMS Podcast, Andrew McCabe's Claim Clinic Podcast as well as The Blue Collar Nation Podcast from Eric Sprague and Larry Wilberton.

Abbreviated Resume:

2002 started with (at that time) the largest national franchise (Ventura, CA) - heavy XM8 & program work, sales, training and team development. Started my property restoration career during the short lived era of "mold is gold".

Local family owned general contractor (Salem, OR) - started restoration division from scratch, no XM8 but good amount of insurance work, sales, training and team development. Good test to see if I could recreate what I learned from my mentor and the success we had. Developing estimating skills outside of Xactimate.

Self employed - no XM8, some insurance work. Time to see if I could build a business on my own. The importance of good estimating, production and profitabilty hits home when it's your own business.

Emerged battered and bruised from The Great Recession to join the largest independently owned international restoration contractor (Eugene, OR) - heavy XM8 & program work, sales, training and team development. I didn't start over, but I wasn't back to pre-recession roles and responsibilities so I had to earn my way back up "the ladder".

Developed an estimating structure for our **contents** division to break our reliance on labor only line items and increased profitability with less resistance from carriers.

Developed an estimating structure for **asbestos abatement** that allowed us to raise the ceiling for this specialty work from 10 & 10 sub-contractor invoices. Our profitability increased, less resitance from carriers and efficiency in the process with our abatement contractors.

Trained new estimators for mitigaton and repairs to grow our team while I was there and ensure its sustained success after my departure.

National restoration contractor that had recently formed from the merging of several prior regional operations (Seattle, WA) - hired to help transition an office with zero program work or experience into competency. Heavy XM8 and program work, sales, training and team development.

Recruited an estimating and project management team from scratch. This included taking someone from another industry and training them to go from zero to hero as a high producing Xactimate estimator. *I have found that training people who are honest, hard-working and willing to learn is always more rewarding, personally and professionally, than trying to train away bad habits.*

Regional abatement contractor (Tacoma, WA) - some XM8 and insurance work, sales.

I f you have found this book to be helpful. Please subscribe to our Youtube as well as via your favorite podcast application (Spotify, Apple, Anchor or Google). The DYOJO Podcast is INFOtainment to help you shorten your DANG learning curve for professional development.

Topics and episodes of The DYOJO Podcast:

Episode 26 - Playing nice in the sandbox (rather than making it a litter box) with Ed Fogle (Baltimore, MD)

Episode 25 - Fear and loathing in social media with Michelle Blevins (Detroit, MI)

Episode 24 - Pro vs. Joe 005 - FOMO your sales and your approach to innovation (Tacoma, WA)

Episode 23 - Uncovering the dark truths of working with adjusters with Kirk Matthews (Salem, OR)

Episode 22 - Growing your business without compromising your values with Lex Sisney (Santa Barbara, CA)

Episode 21 - Pro vs. Joe 004 - Motivating your team with vision (Tacoma, WA)

Episode 20 - Crisis leads to opportunity with Rachel Stewart (Mesa, AZ)

Episode 19 - Leading yourself first so that you can better lead others with Skylar Lewis (Temecula, CA)

Episode 18 - The growing pains of a young business - Pro vs. Joe 003 (Tacoma, WA)

Episode 17 - Train to obtain with Eric "The Tech Whisperer" Sprague of MorningTechMeeting.com (Salt Lake City, UT)

Episode 16 - Doing Good in Your Hood with a panel of guests including Tammy Birklid (Merit Construction), Bryan Reynolds (Anthem Coffee), Rick Dancer (Rick Dancer Media), Gerrett Stier (GMS Podcast) and William Mendoza (Rockland Firewater)

Episode 15 - No risk = No reward with Denis Beaulieu of Alliance Environmental (Thousand Oaks, CA)

Episode 14 - Pro vs. Joe 002 - Powering up with good relationships

Episode 13 - Taking care of your partners with William Mendoza of Rockland Restoration (Bellflower, CA)

Episode 12 - Leadership motivation from real leaders who lead with Mike Kinney of Coppertop Construction (Eugene, OR) and David Smith who is currently recovering from a career in property restoration (Eugene, OR)

Episode 11 - Humor and using Instagram for your business with Water Damage Daily (@waterdamagedaily)

Episode 10 - Pro vs. Joe 001 - Branding fails and networking *New Segment with Bryan Close of All American Real Estate Services (Tacoma, WA)

Episode 9 - Silica sand and the power of humility with Mark Whatley of Actionable Insights (San Diego, CA)

Episode 8 - Extending the life of your restoration equipment with Elan Pasmanick of Born to Repair (San Diego, CA)

Episode 7 - Elevating your mold remediation game with Amy Siedlecki of The Mold Reporters (Portland, OR)

Episode 6 - Communication with insurance carriers with Raymond Tittmann of Tittmann Weix (Los Angeles, CA)

Episode 5 - Innovation is the new normal with Andrew McCabe of Claims Delegates (Bend, OR)

Episode 4 - Facing Adversity as an entrepreneur with Rick Dancer of Rick Dancer Media (Springfield, OR)

Episode 3 - Property restoration law and advocacy with Ed "The Restoration Lawyer" Cross of Edward H Cross & Associates

Episode 2 - Emergency management preparedness and planning with Edward Colson of Ready Northwest (Portland, OR)

Episode 1 - Insurance claims advocacy with David Princeton of Advocate Claim Serivce (WI)

---

[1] The DYOJO Podcast Episode 15 - No Risk, No Reward with Denis Beaulieu of Alliance Environmental is available as a video on Youtube (https://youtu.be/c7ToQ9myie8) and on audio via Spotify, Apple, Anchor and Google (https://thedyojopodcast.com/episodes)

[2] Schoolyard Fences - https://www.sciencedirect.com/science/article/pii/S2095263520300194

[3] TDP Ep. 13 - https://youtu.be/OVBpKGGp6lU

[4] Lessons - https://www.izvents.com/words/lessons

[5] TDP Ep. 20 - https://www.youtube.com/watch?v=db9BZNYpupQ&feature=youtu.be

[6] Proverbs 24:32

[7] Jon Isaacson's monthly column The Intentional Restorer with Restoration and Remediation Magazine (R&R) - https://www.randrmagonline.com/topics/4576-the-intentional-restorer

[8] TDP - www.thedyojopodcast.com

[9] People in a Position of Leadership (PIAPOL) - https://www.izvents.com/words/piapol

[10] The Four P's aka The Blueprint for Success from The DYOJO - https://www.izvents.com/blueprint-for-success.html

[11] The Intentional Restorer is a monthly column with R&R Magazine - https://www.randrmagonline.com/topics/4576-the-intentional-restorer

[12] The DYOJO - www.thedyojo.com

[13] The DYOJO Podcast - www.thedyojopodcast.com

[14] Free E-book - www.izvents.com/ebook

[15] Actionable Inisights - https://www.getinsights.org/resources/insighter-report/xactimate-history-future/

[16] ATI - https://atirestoration.com/

[17] View our "episodes" page on www.thedyojopodcast.com

[18] Pro vs. Joe Podcast - https://www.thedyojopodcast.com/pro-vs-joe.html

[19] OVCCS - https://www.oregonvalleyandcoastal.com/

[20] David was a member of our discussion panel for The DYOJO Podcast Episode 12, Leadership Motivation from Real Leaders Who Lead - https://youtu.be/hiOzO-bZf7c

[21] This book currently does not have a title but you can track our progress on my website - https://www.izvents.com/culture-book.html

[22] Teaching kids the basics of sketching for an Xactimate estimate - https://youtu.be/2h7TKRh__Ho

[23] Actionable Insights - www.getinsights.org

[24] HES - https://www.linkedin.com/in/home-estimating-services-719a82a8

[25] The DYOJO Podcast Episode 5 on Youtube - https://youtu.be/H6XkuX-VEMs

[26] Article - https://www.randrmagonline.com/articles/87287-three-things-estimators-can-do-to-improve-consistency-in-their-restoration-estimates

[27] Common estimating issues taken from Help! Claims Review Shredded My Estimate - https://www.izvents.com/words/shredded-estimates

[28] Four P's of the Blueprint for Success from The DYOJO - www.izvents.com/blueprint-for-success

[29] Pro vs. Joe is a podcast within a podcast from The DYOJO Podcast - https://youtu.be/2YKgH7Tp8IU

[30] https://www.thedyojopodcast.com/pro-vs-joe.html

[31] The Blueprint for Success - www.izvents.com/blueprint-for-success

[32] Article - https://www.izvents.com/words/garbage-pt1

[33] Eliminating chaos in your organization - https://youtu.be/Y-o9lbTvLg4

[34] The DYOJO Podcast Episode 15 with Denis Beaulieu - https://youtu.be/c7ToQ9myie8

[35] Aligning Your Mindset for Executing on Your Leadership Goals - https://www.randrmagonline.com/articles/88922-aligning-your-mindset-for-executing-on-your-leadership-goals

[36] Better Communcation = Better Outcomes - https://youtu.be/J-bW1RN67Hs

[37] Shredded video - https://youtu.be/6XzbaL6Y_Uk

[38] Advanced Xactimate & Pricing Training Classes - https://www.enlightenedrestorationsolutions.com/

[39] Scope Creep (wiki) - https://en.wikipedia.org/wiki/Scope_creep#:~:text=Scope%20creep%20(also%20called%20requirement,defined%2C%20documented%2C%20or%20controlled.

[40] Article - https://www.randrmagonline.com/articles/88874-a-history-of-collaboration-a-future-of-advocacy

[41] Mastering Contents Estimates with Annissa Coy - https://

www.randrmagonline.com/articles/87249-ask-annissa-mastering-contents-estimates

[42] Blue Collar Nation Podcast from Morning Tech Meeting - https://morningtechmeeting.com/

[43] Jeff Bezos - https://www.inc.com/jeff-haden/20-years-ago-jeff-bezos-said-this-1-thing-separates-people-who-achieve-lasting-success-from-those-who-dont.html

[44] EMTA - https://trainemta.com/

[45] Two Questions (article) - https://www.izvents.com/words/am-i-a-leader / (video) - https://youtu.be/btFeHnXX6Mg

[46] Andrew McCabe has a great hashtag #ThickestFileWins which we discuss on The DYOJO Podcast Episode 5 - https://youtu.be/cSFx7VpKiYw

[47] Pricing Estimates - https://www.randrmagonline.com/articles/87592-pricing-estimates-the-bottom-line

[48] RIA Report 3 - https://cr.restorationindustry.org/Full-Article/ArtMID/385/ArticleID/387/Restoration-Advocacy-Report-3

[49] Invest in the RIA's AGA - https://www.restorationindustry.org/page/aga

[50] The three part discussion with Xactware President Mike Fulton is available for viewing by RIA Members on the RIA website - https://www.restorationindustry.org/

[51] AIR - https://airestore.org/

[52] ICRA - http://www.icrassociation.org/

[53] NORRP - https://norrp.org/about-norrp/

[54] TRA - https://www.restorationassociation.com/about

[55] RIA - https://www.restorationindustry.org/

[56] Restoration Rebels - https://www.facebook.com/groups/RestorationRebel/

[57] Ben Franklin - https://contently.net/2014/08/21/voices/frontlines/ben-franklin-taught-write-clever-tricks/

[58] Cover bands - https://www.bbc.co.uk/programmes/articles/38rJrt2ZVRlXCzXCZbBGTlH/ten-huge-bands-who-started-out-as-tribute-or-covers-acts#:~:text=The%20Rolling%20Stones,R%26B%20to%20get%20people%20dancing.

[59] Xactimate price list update - https://www.getinsights.org/resources/price-list-update-summary/

[60] Xactimate training courses - https://www.enlightenedrestorationsolutions.com/page/xactimate-training

[61] Xactware training - https://www.xactware.com/store/TRAINING---by-Type/1-1.do

[62] The DYOJO - https://www.xactware.com/store/TRAINING---by-Type/1-1.do

[63] IAQ Radio - https://www.iaqradio.com/about/

[64] GMS Podcast - https://gmsdist.com/pages/podcast

[65] Blue Collar Nation Radio - https://morningtechmeeting.com/bluecollarradiostation/

[66] The Claim Clinic - https://podcasts.apple.com/us/podcast/the-claim-clinic/id982839824

[67] Straight Talk - https://www.youtube.com/playlist?list=PLR3tWI3apCdAZjwxWhvpYLmBgp8JpQFpU

[68] Brian Hoyer on Tom Brady - https://www.espn.com/blog/new-england-patriots/post/_/id/4816289/tom-brady-spends-time-with-throwing-coach-during-playoff-bye-week

[69] Pro vs. Joe Podcast from The DYOJO Podcast - www.thedyojopodcast.com/pro-vs-joe

[70] We know this quote does not originate with Mr. Whatley - https://youtu.be/s41xyUthN8k

[71] OVCCS - https://www.oregonvalleyandcoastal.com/

[72] Free PDF download - https://www.izvents.com/ebook.html

[73] Michelle Blevins on GMS Podcast - https://open.spotify.com/episode/2OqPt7dJUVbeeeq3PocMbj

[74] Reduce to Produce - https://www.izvents.com/reduce-to-produce.html

[75] Blueprint for Success - https://www.izvents.com/blueprint-for-success.html

[76] Two Questions - https://www.izvents.com/two-questions.html

[77] The Bruce Lee Mindset for Business - https://cleanfax.com/management/bruce-lee-mindset-prioritize-focus/

[78] Review of Unqualified Success - https://www.randrmagonline.com/articles/88591-are-you-ready-to-be-an-unqualified-success

Made in the USA
Columbia, SC
27 August 2020